Handling Rumors and Gossip in Business, the Workplace, and Everyday Life

Sociological Perspectives

Vivencio Ballano

Copyright © 2017 Vivencio Ballano

All rights reserved.

DEDICATION

To my beloved wife, Emily, my daughter, Joanne Faye, and to my only son, Johann Karl. To our Lord Jesus Christ, our Savior.

CONTENTS

Acknowledgments   i

1 Introduction   1

2 The Nature of Rumors and Gossip   5

    2.1. Introduction
    2.2 Rumors and Gossip as Collective Behaviors
    2.3 Defining Rumors and Gossip
    2.4 Some Social Science Definitions of Rumors
    2.5 Understanding Rumors and Gossip
    2.6 Sociological Classification
    2.7 Ten Criteria in Classifying Rumors
    2.8 Rumors in Today's Globalizing World
    2.9 Crisis and Rumors
    2.10 Forms of Rumors
    2.11 Common Circulation Areas of Rumors and Gossip
    2.12 People Prone to Engage in Rumors and Gossip
    2.13 Summary

3 The Social Functions of Rumors and Gossip   29

    3.1 Introduction
    3.2 The Nature of Rumors and Gossip in Daily Life
    3.3 Social Functions of Rumors and Gossip
    3.4 Summary

4 Breeding Ground of Rumors and Gossip   44

    4.1 Introduction
    4.2 Organizational Factors Affecting Rumors and Gossip
    4.3 Rumors and Gossip and Ambiguous Situations
    4.4 Summary

5 Distinguishing the Truth from Lies, Rumors, and Gossip   54

5.1 Introduction
5.2 How to Judge the Truthfulness of Information
5.3 Cultural Differences in Verifying Lying
5.4 Summary

6 Company Rumors   63

6.1 Introduction
6.2 Nature of Company Rumors
6.3 How to Deal with Rumors in the Company
6.4 How to Handle Commercial Rumors
6.5 Legal Approach to Stop Office Rumors
6.6 Summary

7 Social Functions of Rumors and Gossip in Business   75

7.1 Introduction
7.2 Structural Problems Supporting Rumors and Gossip
7.3 Summary

8 Critical Advice on How to Deal with Rumors and Gossip   89

8.1 Introduction
8.2 Advice on Physical Appearance
8.3 Advice concerning Personal Trait and Practice
8.4 Summary

ACKNOWLEDGMENTS

This book on rumors and gossip would not have been possible without the generous help and inspiration of the following persons:

To Dr. Ricardo G. Abad,
Chairperson of the Sociology-Anthropology
Department at the Ateneo de Manila University,
my wise advisor and friend throughout my sociological training,
for his continuous support and inspiration;

To all my followers on LinkedIn and social media, for reading and liking my posts on rumors and gossip online that led to the publication of this book;

To my wife, Emily, and my children, Joanne Faye and Johann Karl, for their loving support and inspiration.

Above all, to our Lord Jesus and Mama Mary, for the blessings and guidance in my apostolate of writing, my own way of serving the Church and society.

1 INTRODUCTION

Homer Simpson in The Simpsons says: "Don't tell a lie! It takes two to lie. One to lie and one to listen." In Christian Ethics, lying is the giving of wrong information to the person or group who has the right to know the truth, just as a debtor informing his/her creditor that s/he can't pay the debt because s/he is broke when, in fact, s/he has money and just doesn't want to pay. A daughter is also lying if she told her parents that she already paid the money intended for the school when in fact she spent it personally; or finally, a recruiter saying nice things to applicants about the hiring company's benefits when in fact they don't exist. Lying happens when what people say and do outwardly do not correspond exactly to with what they think with the intention to deceive others.

Spreading rumors and gossip is a form of lying in a sense that what is being shared by the rumormonger or gossip is inaccurate or false and thus deceives people who deserve to know the truth. A rumor or gossip can be a complete lie if the content is a pure invention with no factual basis. But it can also be a half-truth if only a portion of the story or information is false. In this case, a rumor or gossip can be a subtle form of lying which requires the listener to figure out which part of the information is correct and which one is false.

Not all rumors and gossip are, however, destructive to people's honor. Some are jokes and incredible tales which are intended by people to entertain friends. But others are slanderous and libelous that torment and dishonor people and organizations. These types of rumors and gossip can be aptly be labeled as "weapons of mass destruction" and can be considered as one of the most destructive forces in the face of the earth. They can destroy people's daily lives, careers, businesses, and futures. And no one is immune from this reality, not even the rich, the famous, and the powerful.

Nasty rumors and gossip do not just "kill" people psychologically due to loss of honor and public shaming but also literally due to depression and suicide. Teenage suicide in the U.S., for instance, is on the rise because of the use of humiliating e-gossip and rumors in cyberbullying. Bullies use rumors and gossip to humiliate their vulnerable targets whether in real life or in cyberspace. Two girls, for instance, were arrested in connection with the death of 12-year-old Rebecca Sedwick, who committed suicide after being the target of online bullying, receiving online messages calling her "ugly," telling her to "drink bleach and die" and encouraging her to kill herself. One of these bullies even boasted on Facebook after Rebecca's suicide that she bullied Rebecca and she didn't care at all if she committed suicide.[1]

People may underestimate the power of unverified information. But rumors and gossip do not only destroy people's lives but also large organizations such as empires. The famous Han Dynasty which was considered as the golden age in Chinese history, for instance, collapsed in 220-221 CE because of the circulation of rumors by the empire's enemies which eventually resulted in the non-payment of tax and shortage of revenues to maintain the empire. Peasants were said to flee and scatter themselves in the villages to avoid the dynasty's tax collectors. They used rumors as an early-warning device to avoid paying taxes.[2] The collapse of the German Empire in 1918 was also precipitated by anti-dynasty rumors circulated by enemy agents.

Rumors and gossip can also shake the operation of big business

---

[1]http://www.dailymail.co.uk/news/article-2511202/Katelyn-Roman-accused-bullying-Rebecca-Sedwick- did-wrong.html.

[2]http://asianhistory.about.com/od/ancientchina/f/Why-Did-Han-China-Collapse.htm.

organizations. Oreo, the America's favorite chocolate cookies with the cream center, for example, was forced to change the colors of their cookies after rumors of racist behavior were hurled by some people against the firm. Rumor mongers alleged that the firm's cookies were representative of two black men sexually assaulting a white woman as symbolized by Oreo's chocolate cookies with a white cream in the middle. Because of serious threats against its headquarters and factories, Oreo changed the colors of their cookies from dark black to lightly-toned magenta to eliminate the rumors.[3]

Finally, rumors and gossip can influence global economic affairs. One report, for instance, blamed rumors for the dramatic slide of the oil price decline in June 2014. Usually, the sharp price rise or increase is in response to war or natural disasters. But the sharp drop in late 2014 – when crude oil prices fell from a high of $115 a barrel in June 2014 to a low of $45 a barrel in January 2015 was said to be largely caused by rumors and speculations in the price wars between oil-exporting countries.[4] With today's digital technology and social media, rumors and gossip can easily become viral and global and thus affect world affairs. Indeed, no one is spared from the insidious snares of intrigues, hoaxes, urban legends and other forms of unverified information. It is, therefore, necessary to create a sort of a critical guide from a sociological perspective, to help people on how to understand and handle rumors and gossip in business and everyday life to avoid or minimize personal and corporate "destruction". Through its "sociological imagination" (C. Wright Mills) or holistic thinking, the sociological approach aims to see the connections between what's happening between the individual and society, biography and history, and the micro and the macro.

This book is divided into eight chapters. Chapter 1 provides an introduction of the book and an overview on the nature of rumors and gossip. Chapter 2 discusses the nature of rumors and gossip.

---

[3] http://empirenews.net/oreo-to-change-color-of-cookies-to-combat-rumors-of-racism/.

[4] http://www.usnews.com/news/blogs/at-the-edge/2015/03/24/rumors-fuel-oil-price-decline.

Chapter 3 explains the important social functions of rumors and gossip in society. distinguishes the truth from rumors from gossip. Chapter 4 identifies the most common breeding ground for rumors and gossip. Chapter 5 distinguishes the truth from rumors and gossip. Chapter 6 deals with company rumors. Chapter 7 discusses the important social functions of rumors and gossip in business. Finally, Chapter 8 provides some critical advice on how to handle rumors and gossip in business and daily life. To reach out a wider audience, it incorporates some popular news stories about rumor and gossip on the life of some celebrities, business leaders and personalities as cases or examples to illustrate how rumors and gossip work in actual social settings. The blueprint of this book is based on my LinkedIn post entitled "How to Handle Rumors and Gossips in Business or Public Life" which generated more than 26K+ views (and still continues to be searched and viewed online). One viewer even considered this post as one of his favorite articles on business management. The positive feedback about this post as well as the scarcity of social scientists writing on rumors and gossip have encouraged me to write this book in order to help people and organizations that suffered much because of unverified information.

2 THE NATURE OF RUMORS AND GOSSIP

2.1 Introduction

This chapter discusses the nature of rumors and gossip as a collective behavior. It explains why rumors and gossip are created and circulated by people, how they are used as tools of domination and social resistance by the powerful and the weak, and what type of people who are most likely to spread unverified information in corporate and everyday life, both in the realm of personal and digital social interactions. It clarifies the fundamental difference between a rumor and gossip as well as identifies other forms of unverified information such as intrigue, hoax, urban legend, and speculation. In general, a rumor deals with social issues while gossip deals with personalities and personal traits. This chapter ends with a summary.

2.2 Rumors and Gossip as Collective Behaviors

Nobody seems to have been the subject of more rumors than Michael Jackson. While still alive, Jackson was rumored to be involved in child molestation, sleeping in an oxygen chamber and undertook plastic surgery to make himself look whiter. People of "royal blood" are not also spared from rumors and gossip. Prince Charles, the heir to the British throne, for instance, is often a victim of all sorts of rumors and gossip. The weirdest of them all is that Charles eats seven hard-boiled eggs for breakfast. A gossip that turned out to be false. The British prince actually went out of his way to debunk this on his website.[5] Finally, not even the mother of the boxing icon Manny Pacquiao is immune from rumors and gossip. In the Philippines, a rumor is circulating that Pacquiao always wins his fights whenever his mother Mommy Dionesia attends his boxing match. Mommy Dionesia allegedly performs some secret prayers or rituals which can weaken his son's opponent. This rumor is, of course, ridiculous as Pacquiao lost to Mayweather even if his mother was present during the fight of the century last May 2, 2015. So, what kind of behavior is rumors and gossip? Why do they seem to emerge from nowhere?

A rumor or gossip in Sociology is a form of collective behavior. A collective behavior does not originate from an ordinary individual or group behavior but from a collectivity. Unlike an ordinary group behavior, a collective behavior has no definite social patterns, although directed towards a common goal. In a panic flight, for instance, the behavior of an individual in a group can be unpredictable but it follows a similar and parallel pattern with that of others and is directed toward the same goal—to escape a dangerous situation. Panic is driven by people's fear of danger and need for self-preservation. A chaotic escape of movie goers inside a cinema because of fire is an example of a collective behavior of panic.

A collective behavior is a type of action that is bizarre, unusual or unique that takes place only on a sporadic and haphazard basis. Sociologists define collective behavior as a "relatively spontaneous and temporary behavior that involves a large number of people engaging in activities that violate conventional norms."[6] Turner and Killian (1987) defined it as "those forms of social behavior in which usual conventions cease to guide social action and people collectively transcend, bypass, or subvert established institutional patterns and

---

[5]http://akorra.com/2012/11/23/top-ten-people-destroyed-by-rumors/.

[6]Monnier, C (Ed.) "What is Collective Behavior".http//:www.globalsociology.pbworks.com.

structures".⁷ It is a spontaneous and unstructured behavior of a group of people in response to the same event, situation, or problem, such as panic, riot or mob. Those who engage in collective behavior are considered by sociologists as a collectivity, a more transitory category that refers to a large group of people characterized by a limited interaction, loyalty, and division of labor. A collectivity, for sociologists, can either be localized, i.e., the members are in one another's physical proximity such as a crowd, or dispersed, i.e, the members of the collectivity are not proximate to one another but have an impact on another's behavior such as rumors and gossip.⁸ Other forms of collective behavior include panics, fads, crazes, disaster behavior, social movement, and other unique events. Rumors and gossip are dispersed type of collective behavior which are unstructured and spontaneous. Thus, they can be unpredictable and difficult to control. Without a sufficient understanding of their social dynamics, people can easily become victims of bullying and defamation.

2.3 Defining Rumors and Gossip

As a collective behavior, a rumor can be defined as a piece of information gathered informally that is used to interpret an ambiguous situation.⁹ It is a "rapidly spreading report unsubstantiated by authenticated fact."¹⁰ It is also considered as news that is presumed to be true without being confirmed or made evident by the person or group which circulated them. Thus, a rumor is an unverified piece of information or story about a subject that is created and spread by people informally by word-of-mouth or

---

⁷ Turner, R. & Killian, L.M. (1987). *Collective Behavior*. Canada: Pearson Education, p.3.

⁸ Ibid.

⁹ Schaefer, R. (2005). *Sociology*. New York: McGraw-Hill.

¹⁰ Horton, T. R. (1983). Rumors: A corporate communication crisis. *Security Management,* 27(6), p.386. Retrieved from http://search.proquest.com/docview/231188092?accountid=33657.

through social media and other electronic means to explain a situation where accurate information is absent or lacking. Thus, if the release of salary for the employees on a payday is delayed considerably without prior notice from the company, rumors are expected to surface and circulate to explain why this incident occurred. The employees themselves would start to think of explanations or theories on why this incident happened in order to take some sort of control on this ambiguous situation. This can also happen in school if a scheduled meeting is canceled without prior notice by school administrators. One must remember that rumors thrive in ambiguous situations in which people are looking for clear and credible information.

Like a rumor, a gossip is another form of collective behavior. It is defined as "a private conversation between two people about someone else who is not around. The information they are discussing is represented as factual, even though, the truth may not have been confirmed."[11] A gossip usually deals with personal matters or traits such as sexual orientation, hidden immoral act, undesirable personal attitude or an embarrassing physical defect or disability.

2.4 Some Social Science Definitions of Rumors

The sociologist Shibutani (1966) defined rumor as a recurrent form of communication through which people attempt to construct a meaningful or working interpretation of a threatening or ambiguous situation by pooling their intellectual resources.[12]

The most common rumor stereotype holds that the content of rumors is highly inaccurate, distorted, and exaggerated. But "evidence from empirical research clearly indicates that assertions about the inaccuracy of rumors are not warranted. Rumors are not always inaccurate, nor do they necessarily grow increasingly distorted. In his

---

[11] http://education-portal.com.

[12] Shibutani, T. (1966). *Improvised News: a sociological study of rumor*. New York: The Bobbs-Merril Company, Inc., p. 17.

comprehensive review of the literature, David Miller (1985) concluded that although some rumors were false, the vast majority proved to be accurate and not distorted.[13]

To cope with incomplete information and uncertain situations, people resort to rumors. Thus, rumors can be considered as what Shibutani (1966) calls as improvised news.[14] There will be no problem if all rumors are false. The public would just immediately dismissed them. However, not all rumors are false. Some contain partial truths that affect business. In one study, for instance, 43% of merger rumors published in the "Hear on the Street" column in the *The Wall Street Journal* turned out to be accurate.[15]

The popular understanding of rumor is that it is talk that is unsubstantiated by authority or evidence as to its veracity.[16] The term is often synonymous with lie or hoax. However scholars use the concept differently. Rumors are neither inherently true or false. Rather as a distinct category of information, it refers to sources that lack direct access to access secure and definite knowledge. Rumors are tentative and unverified claims. Rumors are like hypotheses (unconfirmed propositions) whereby message transmission takes place in such a way that the hearer does not quite know whether or not to believe the message.[17] They are similar to research hypotheses

---

[13] Miller, D. (1985). *Introduction to Collective Behavior.* Bermont, CA: Wadsworth, p.512.

[14] Shibutani, T. (1966). *Improvised News: a sociological study of rumor.* New York: The Bobbs-Merril Company, Inc.

[15] Fine, G. A., & Difonzo, N. (2011, Summer). Uncertain knowledge. *Contexts, 10,* p.18.

[16] Ben-Ze'eb, A. (1994)."The Vindication of Gossip", in Goodman, R.F. and Ben-Ze'eb (Eds.). Good Gossip. University Press of Kansas, Lawrence KS, p.p. 11-22.

[17] Rosnow, R.L. (1988). "Rumors as Communication: a contextualist approach. *Journal of Communication.* Vol. 38. No. 1, pp. 12-28.

in a scientific studies in a sense that they are tentative assertions of social phenomena which can neither true or false. They needs confirmation from data or evidence to support their claims. Thus, a hypothesis, for instance, which says that high poverty incidence can lead to crimes is neither true or false, depending on evidence or data. If the findings of a study show that it is not poverty but lax enforcement of laws that primarily caused crimes, then the hypothesis is false. But if a study can show that it is primarily the high level of poverty in a particular locality that caused the high level of crime, then the hypothesis is true. Rumors can be compared by analogy to hypotheses. They are tentative propositions of ambiguous situations that need empirical support. Fine and DiFonso (2011: 18) call rumors as "folk hypotheses" that explain shared concerns and manage common threats" that need verification and factual evidence.[18] Rumors are "improvised news" (Shibutani, 1966) when no reliable and accurate news of ambiguous situations are available.[19]

Rumors are interpreted according to people's biases and undergo filtering. In Davis' rumor model (1952), individuals receive and transmit rumors in terms of their own biases. Although the essential content is retained, rumors undergo filtering where individuals add or reduce some of their details in order to pursue their personal interests.[20]

2.5 Understanding Rumors and Gossip

People tend to use the term rumor and gossip interchangeably in ordinary conversation or reporting. But academic disciples tend to define and describe them differently. Despite the variety of

---

[18] Fine, G. A., & Difonzo, N. (2011, Summer). Uncertain knowledge. *Contexts, 10*, **p.18**.

[19] Shibutani, T. (1966). *Improvised News: a sociological study of rumor.* New York: The Bobbs-Merril Company, Inc.

[20] Akanda, A., & Odewale, F. (1994). Company rumor: The fact and fiction. *Employment Bulletin and IR Digest, 10*(3), 1.

definitions, many agree that both rumor and gossip are unverified information. They can be completely or partially true or false. There is also a basic difference between rumors and gossip: Rumors are more focused on social issues or matters that affect the common good of a group or community while gossip is focused on personal issues and traits of particular people or personalities. Thus, one main difference between a rumor and gossip is on their content. If it deals with social issues that affect the common good of a group or society, then it is a rumor. If it only deals with personal matters and affecting one person or a few individuals, then it is a gossip. A rumor, therefore, affects a group's communal good while a gossip affects only an individual's well being. A rumor can, thus, affect an entire organization, school, institution or society, but a gossip can only affect a particular manager, teacher, student or individual. If a particular company is maligned by people using unverified information, it is not a gossip, but a rumor since it affects the entire firm. At times, however, rumors and gossip can overlap with one another since there is a thin line that separates these two. A manager, for instance, who occupies a top position in the company and is being gossiped for wrongdoing can probably generate rumors if his or her act can affect the welfare of the entire organization. Thus, a company president who is gossiped to be a womanizer and corrupt can generate a rumor that the company would soon be bankrupt as corporate funds were used to maintain his or her expensive extramarital affairs.

A rumor, as well as a gossip, can turn out to be true, although it may not always be exactly as contained in their information. The truthfulness of a rumor does not, however, licensed anyone to reveal and disseminate the information without the consent of the person or party concerned. This can violate the person's right to privacy and can be libelous especially if there is malice and published in the broadcast, print or social media.

2.6 Sociological Classification

P. Sorokin (1991) classifies rumors in accordance to social elements of interaction systems: the quality and quantity of communicating (interacting) individuals, type of interaction and character of information conveyors. This classification seems to be more sociological because it enables to identify which groups spread rumors and how they do it. However, this classification does not mention other important things such as the content of rumors and their relation to reality and so on.

The American sociologists W. A. Peterson and N. P. Gist (1951) classify rumors into types according to their content (political, economic, etc.), time orientation (explaining past, predictive or foretelling), origin (spontaneous, purposive) or relation with reality (rational, fantastic).[21]

With regard to content, rumors can be classified into four types:[22]

2.6.1 "Pipe dream" or Wish Fulfillment

These rumors largely express the hopes of those who circulate them such expressing a possible solution to a work problem that employee wants to change.

2.6.2 "Bogey" or Anxiety Rumor

These are primarily driven by fear, and, consequently, create unease among its recipients such as rumors of job layoffs.

2.6.3 Anticipatory Rumor

Precipitated by ambiguous situations, these rumors try to resolve uncertainty by anticipating future events such as a rumor of who would be the next president of the company or whether he or she

---

[21] Peterson, W.A., & N.P. Gist (1951): Rumor and public opinion, American Journal of Sociology, 45, 159–167.

[22] Michelson, G, & Mouly, V.S. (2004). Do Loose Lips Sink?: The meaning, antecedents, and consequences of rumour and gossip in organisations. *Corporate Communications: An International Journal.* 9 (3): 189-201.

would come from within or outside the company.

2.6.4 Aggressive Rumor

These malicious rumors which are motivated to harm the reputation of others or business competitors. The famous worm rumor for McDonald's is a classic example for this. The American clothing designer, Tommy Hilfiger was also a victim of aggressive false rumor. "It was a shocking story that had circulated for years on the Internet and through the word of mouth that Hilfiger, known for his colorful, preppy styles, had supposedly appeared on the *The Oprah Winfrey Show* to air a disturbing grievance."If I had known that African-Americans, Hispanics, and Asians would buy my clothes, I would not have made them so nice, " Hilfiger complained. "I wish those people would buy my clothes—they were made for upper-class whites." According to the tale, an outraged Winfrey immediately asked Hilfiger to leave her show—and when she came back from a commercial, he was gone." Of course, Hilfiger had never said anything of the sort. At the time the rumor surfaced and spread, Hilfiger had never been on *The Oprah Winfrey Show*. It fact the two had never met. Only after the spread of the rumor that Hilfiger was invited by Oprah to the show to squelch the rumor once and for all.[23]

A typology of rumors is constructed according to their relation to reality after their veracity has been authenticated. True rumors become information. Untrue rumors are categorized as affirming or denying rumors; affirming rumors state the reality of imaginary facts, whereas denying rumors undermine the reality of established facts.[24]

2.7 Ten Criteria in Classifying Rumors

---

[23] Clark, T., & Dixit, J. (2008). The 8 ½ Laws of Rumor Spread. *Psychology Today,* 41, 80-86,8. Retrieved from http://search.proquest.com/docview/214475416?accountid=33657.

[24] Renard J. (2007). Denying rumors. *Diogenes.* 54 (1): 43–58.

Although the various classifications of rumors by scholars, P. Valdas (2008) believes that every rumor despite its topics has certain features which can be set using a particular system of criteria which can describe a rumor and name the peculiarities of its functioning and spread. To define any rumor, it is important to include the following ten criteria:

1. Social actualness of a rumor (actual and unreal),
2. Purpose of a rumor (popular, unpopular),
3. Nature of a rumor (malicious or entertaining (jokes)
4. Depth of a rumor (superficial or deep),
5. Supplier (author) of a rumor (known, authoritative or unknown),
6. Receiver of a rumor (activist or amateur)
7. Object of rumor contents (individuals, social groups, institutions),
8. Area of rumor spread (country, region, village, social group, professional group),
9. Duration of rumor existence (short-lived, long-lived)
10. Restrictions of rumor spread (juridical and moral sanctions for spreading the rumor or absence of them).[25]

2.8 Rumors in Today's Globalizing World

Rumors are usually thought of to flourish in an environment of news blackouts and information famines and thus, assumed to diminish in an era of information overload. But the opposite seems to be the case. In contemporary information society, rumors seem to arise not from lack of information but from an information overload.[26] In today's globalization age characterized by liquidity and flows, information has become "liquid" and can swiftly penetrate the

---

[25] Valdas, P. (2009). Purpose and Vitality of Rumors: Political Aspects. *Santalka. Filosofija.* 2009, t.17, nr. 1. ISSN 1822-430X print/1822-4318 online. DOI: 10.3846/1822-430X.2009.17.1.29-40.

[26] Kimmel, A. (2003). *Rumors and Rumor Control: A Manager's Guide to Understanding and Combatting Rumors.* Routledge Communication Series.

various domains of social life.[27] Liquidity is a metaphor used by some globalists to explain the growing flexibility and mobility of things that is brought about by the current processes of globalization. Liquidity simply means that things, information and places are increasingly becoming light and thus easy to move from one location to another. Like water, "liquids" can easily "flow" to different locations with the capacity to change their form in order to adapt to the environment. With today's globalization and technological innovation, almost all things have become so fluid and light that they travel in various spaces in blinding speed. In similar manner, news, "fake news," "alternative facts," e-rumors, e-gossip, and other forms of content now mounted in digital and electronic platforms in the cyberspace flow like running water or liquid that penetrates dimensions almost all dimensions of social life. Corporate organizations are not spared from this tsunami of information that besiege the market and the workplace.

As information are easily and freely created, traded, edited, and manipulated to suit one's interests, the veracity of their content declines resulting in the difficulty to know which news are "real," "fake," or "improvised" such as rumors and gossip. With information overload and the constant bombardment of the mind with unverified information from the Internet, people are deprived of the luxury of time and immediate means to swiftly investigate whether the posts, news or information they received from and passed on to other people are totally or partially true or false. This also happens during crisis or emergency situations when information is absent or lacking to ascertain the truth. Knowledge means control. In business settings, sufficient information is good for managers and the corporate organizations they handle to achieve higher productivity and profit.

Rumors and gossip do not normally emerge in moments of certainty where the corporate organization runs smoothly but usually during times of crisis and unexpected change in the day-to-day operations of the company. Thus, rumors usually abound when a

---

[27] Ritzer, G. (2010). *Globalization: A Basic Text*. West Sussex, UK: John Wiley & Sons Ltd.

business firm faces or experiences bankruptcy, leadership change, mergers, buyouts, financial losses, labor problems or restructuring. For instance, when Twitter faces a buyout by other firms, rumors spread like a wildfire. When news was leaked on Twitter will be the takeover target of the giant companies in September 2016, whispers were immediately and spread in the cyberspace. News spread that the engine company Google (Google parent Alphabet (GOOGL, Tech30), would take over the company, pushing the stock value of Twitter to 20% rise. But since no immediate confirmation came from Google, more speculations arise. CNBC mentioned that the business software company Salesforce.com might also be looking to buy Twitter but no clarification what benefits Twitter would bring to this transaction. Later, another rumors surfaced that Verizon (VZ, Tech30) might be bidding for Twitter as well, but Verizon denied the speculation. Since no accurate information to rely on of who would buy Twitter, the rumors continued. The Media companies News Corp (NWSA) and 21st Century Fox (FOXA) -- both controlled by Rupert Murdoch -- have been cited as possible Twitter acquirers too. So has NBC parent company Comcast (CMCSA) as well as the Saudi Prince Alwaleed bin Talal and former Microsoft CEO Steve Ballmer -- who are two of Twitter's largest shareholders -- could team up to take the company private. Again, in the absence of certainty, more rumors surfaced saying that the influential Silicon Valley investors Marc Andreessen and Silver Lake Partners could team up to buy Twitter and so on (La Monica, 2016, 23 Sep). This case of Twitter buyout shows that rumors can immediately spin and become uncontrollable if no convincing and reliable information is available.

The sociologist Tomatsu Shibutani (1966) notes that rumors arise from uncertainty, from the absence of context and concrete information by which those affected by a crisis may understand its significance: "When activity is interrupted for want of adequate information, frustrated [people] must piece together some kind of definition, and rumor is the collective transaction through which they try to fill this gap. Far from being pathological, rumor is part and parcel of the efforts of [people] to come to terms with the exigencies of life."[28] Thus, rumors for Shibutani (1966) are "improvised news,"

---

[28] Doorley, J., & Garcia, H. F. (2007). Rumor has it: Understanding

a tentative information created by people who are affected by uncertainty in order to gain control and to make sense of ambiguous situations or crises.

2.9 Crisis and Rumors

Because crises are characteristically uncertain, rumors are a fact of life. People usually turn to media for guidance to know what happened, what is happening, and what might happen. But the news media, at times, can fail in performing their gatekeeping function. During major crises, especially during its initial stage, such as the September 11 attacks, Lasorsa (2003) noted that the news media's traditional gatekeeping function disintegrates, thus resulting in proliferation of rumors. A major disaster or crisis can almost eliminate gatekeeping role of print and broadcast media. Rumor and disinformation are passed along side accurate reports.[29] In a crisis situation such as the terrorist attack or massive hacking of a large company such as Sony, there is often less time for accuracy during the event. Accuracy and speed of delivery of accurate reports can become acute during crises leading to a floodgate of unverified information. And investigating the accuracy and source of unverified information proved to be difficult. Dealing with rumors can be challenging task as it is hard to figure out where a rumor started, how it is building momentum, and where it might end. In a business setting, once a rumor starts it can easily spread among employees, customers, suppliers, lenders, investors and regulators. It can also feed other existing rumors. And once it reaches the media, the rumor can be formalized and seen by people as accurate renderings of reality.[30]

---

and managing rumors. *Public Relations Strategist, 13*(3), 27-31.

[29] Larosa, D. (2003).News media perpetuate few rumors about 9/11 crisis. *Newspaper Research Journal,* 24, 10-12.

[30] Doorley, J., & Garcia, H. F. (2007). Rumor has it: Understanding and managing rumors. *Public Relations Strategist, 13*(3), 27-31.

2.10 Forms of Rumors

Unverified stories such as rumors and gossip can take different forms and names such as intrigue, hoax, urban legend or speculation. These forms of information all share the same nature as rumors and gossip: tentative, unreliable, and of convincing evidence. They continue to exist because, like rumors and gossip, they serve some social functions in a social organization or society.

2.10.1 Intrigue

Intrigue, as a form of rumor, is something that is done secretly through plotting.[31] It is a secret plot against a leader, person, or group. Its content is usually appealing to other people's curiosity, fancy, or interest.[32] It is associated with power and politics in a social organization. It is usually used as a tool to grab power or to put down a person or group in an organization. In office politics, intrigues are used to undermine the leadership of the manager or to stab other employees in their back.

2.10.2 Hoax

A hoax is a deliberately fabricated falsehood made to masquerade as truth.[33] A hoax can also be defined as "an act of deception which is designed to trick people into believing or doing something. Many are designed as lighthearted practical jokes, although have a more serious purpose, and are intended to raise awareness about an issue or to get a community actively involved in something".[34] Others are really intended to deceive and take

---

[31] http://www.yourdictionary.com/intrigue.

[32] http://dictionary.reference.com/browse/intrigue.

[33] http://en.wikipedia.org/wiki/Hoax.

[34] http://www.ranker.com/list/list-of-celebrity-death-hoaxes/celebrity-lists.

advantage of people such as scams and other forms of deception.

The most common type of hoax on the internet and social are death hoaxes of celebrities. In 2013, Megan Fox, for instance, was the victim of a death hoax in which it was rumored she had been killed in a car crash.13 President Barack Obama too has a death hoax.

2.10.3 Urban Legend

An urban legend is a form of modern folklore consisting of stories that may or may not have been believed by their tellers to be true and often possess horror implications that are believable to their audience. Although the story is called "urban" legend, it does not necessarily mean that they emanate from cities or urban centers. Urban legends can also originate and circulate in rural areas. The term "urban" is just used to differentiate modern or contemporary legends from the traditional legends or folklore of pre-industrial times. That is why sociologists and folklorists prefer the term "contemporary legend" rather than "urban legend."[35]

Like rumor and gossip, an urban legend's veracity is difficult to verify. They are usually passed on by word of mouth or through digital media such as email. Moreover, their contents often use the famous "it happened to a friend of a friend" (or FOAF) clause that makes finding the original source of the story virtually impossible."[36]

Although urban legends may not look credible to educated and mature people, they are, nevertheless, more engaging and attention grabbing; thus, encourage listening. The narrative or story form of urban legends with their sense of mystery, humor or danger often fascinates and intrigues people. So, despite their lack of credibility, people continue to listen and share them.[37]

---

[35] http://en.wikipedia.org/wiki/Urban_legend.

[36] http://www.livescience.com/7107-urban-legends-start-persist.html.
[37] Guerin, B. & Miyazaki, Y. (2006). Analyzing Rumors, Gossip, and Urban Legends through their Conversational Properties. *The Psychological Record*. 2006, 56, 23-34.

Here are some examples of urban legends:

Example 1: Bloody Mary

One of the most popular urban legends for school age children having sleepovers. According to this myth, a person turns out the lights, look into a mirror, and say Bloody Mary three times (in some versions the number of times differs), s/he will summon the spirit of Mary Worth, a woman who was supposedly executed for being a witch.[38]

Example 2: "Cokelore"

There are numerous urban legends involving Coca Cola. In fact, there are so many that these legends all now have their own category known as "Colklore". The most popular is that if you were to leave a tooth in a cup of coke overnight by morning the tooth would be completely dissolved. Like most of the other legends involving the popular drink, this is totally untrue.[39]

Example 3: The Urban Legend on the Giant Alligators of New York City. Are there giant alligators in the sewers of New York City?

Did you know there are giant albino alligators living in the sewers of New York City? No, really! They started out as pets, then got flushed down the toilet when they grew too large for their owners to handle. Or so they say....[40]

2.10.4 Speculation

A speculation is the forming of a theory or conjecture without firm evidence. A theory is a tentative explanation of a social

---

[38] http://list25.com/25-most-popular-urban-legends-still-being-told/.

[39] http://list25.com/25-most-popular-urban-legends-still-being-told/.
[40] http://urbanlegends.about.com/od/classics/.

phenomenon. Let's say a company experienced an unscheduled brownout. In search of an immediate answer why the electricity was lost, employees and managers may start to speculate or theorize without first verifying the cause. Some employee may speculate that the company did pay the electricity bills, thus the electric company cut off the service. Others might speculate that there were problems in the transmission lines, and so on and so forth. All these are speculations and theories. They are not supported by scientific data. If it is proven that the company failed to pay the bills on time and so the electric company cut off the service, this speculation becomes the truth and reality of the cause of the power outage. A theory or speculation is neither true or false. It is the data which can confirm whether it's true or false. A speculation is a theory-construction activity of the mind which try to interpret or explain an existing social phenomenon. Since it is not immediately supported by scientific evidence or data, speculations are forms of unverified information and can be categorized as rumors when passed on by word of mouth or through the social media.

A stock market speculation is an example of a speculative type of rumor. Stock market speculation happens when an investor purchases a stock because he believes the price will go up or down with very little consideration to the value of the stock or the company who issues the stock. The investor then hypothesizes that a particular company will increase or decrease its share price depending on his/her knowledge of the external factors which s/he believes as affecting the firm's stock price. These factors can include a company facing government fines or regulations, approval of a new pharmaceutical drug, merger or acquisition with another company, or high competitive risk.[41]

Speculations may also include some guessing games of who would the next manager, president or CEO of the company, or who would be promoted or retrenched. In speculation, people usually have some evidence, clues or leads about the impending reality, albeit unreliable since no actual and scientific investigation or research has been done yet.

---

[41] http://www.wisegeek.com/what-is-stock-market-speculation.htm.

2.11 Common Circulation Areas of Rumors and Gossip

Before the digital era, the most common way to circulate rumors and gossip is through a verbal exchange in real life or writing in the print media. But with the advent of the Internet and the social media, rumors and gossip now have new platform—the cyberspace. Through Information Communication Technologies (ICT's), rumors and gossip can now be swiftly disseminated through calls, text messages, chats, posts, videos, emails and other digital means. The use of digital media in spreading rumors and gossip are more convenient to perform and more powerful in impact due to wider circulation than face-to-face interaction and traditional media.

Rumors and gossip can be practically everywhere, whether in real time and space or in the virtual or cyberspace of the internet. As long as there are people or online users who are willing to hear them. In face-to-face interaction, the sharing of rumors and gossip usually occurs in inner circles of people such as friends, relatives, office mates, classmates, teammates, etc. But this is different in the cyberspace where social networks can easily merge such connecting one's Facebook, YouTube, Twitter, Pinterest, Instagram and other social media sites into one big network. New apps and sites are emerging that even makes sharing much easier, faster and more convenient. Thus, rumors and gossip can easily fly and immediately shared infinitely in the cyberspace. And they cannot easily be deleted as the internet has no delete button. So what is posted on the Web stays there forever, removing them would require a very tedious process.

Rumors and gossip can be created and shared through chats, emails, online videos, and other digital media. Unlike face-to-face interaction, virtual sharing of rumors and gossip removes the physical obstacles of distance and geographical limitations. In the cyberspace, one only needs to push the share button to spread the rumors and gossip across the globe! E-rumors and e-gossip are faster than the verbal rumor and gossip. The digital platform moves rumors and gossip in a lightning speed which can greatly affect business and people.

2.12 People Prone to Engage in Rumors and Gossip

It is inaccurate to assume that people would always pass circulate a rumor or gossip that they receive from others. Not all people circulate an unverified story to others. Aside from the nature of the content, the decision to pass on a rumor or gossip largely depends on the person's level of education and scientific training, value system, patterns of likes and dislikes and the type of community or organization.

The content of the rumors and gossip, as well as demographics, plays an important role in determining who would most likely share a particular rumors or gossip. It's erroneous to assume that all people would share a popular and intriguing rumor or gossip immediately as soon as they receive them. Highly religious people, for instance, would less likely share a rumor or gossip because of their strong sense of service and respect for human dignity. Top corporate individuals or highly successful people too may not also be inclined to listen to intrigues, rumors and gossip because of their preoccupation to succeed and excel in their endeavors. The highly rational, efficient and supportive organizational culture of these career-oriented people also contribute a lot in shaping their success-oriented minds.

Rumors and gossip are also class-based. There are types of rumors and gossip which may appeal a particular class but not to other classes. The rich and the poor do have different cultural taste and concern that they choose which rumor or gossip to listen and share. So also gender, there are gossips or topics that interest women, but not to men, gays, lesbians or transgender. Social groups are usually united under some common interest. Any talk which does not concern the group's interest may surely be ignored as a waste of time.

Despite demographic differentiation, there is one topic of rumor and gossip which can easily attract people's attention across social classes especially in today's digital— sex. Rumors and gossip about sex scandals or innuendos on people who are expected to be role models or leaders usually appeal to many people. Gossip about the extramarital affairs of politicians and public figures usually go viral in social circles and the internet. Stories about Bill Clinton's sexual affairs with Monica Lewinsky, for instance, are among the high-profile rumors and gossip in U.S. history that nearly led to a presidential impeachment. If this has happened in today's social media age, the impact could have magnified a hundred times. The Democrat vice-presidential hopeful was also forced to withdraw from the political race after a nasty gossip that he had extramarital affairs and a child with a filmmaker he hired for his presidential campaign. Being indiscreet in one's sexual life, especially if one is occupying a position of power and authority is a sure way to salacious gossip and perdition in today's digital age.

By demographics, here are some of the most common type of people who are more likely to create and/or share rumors and gossip. The following only suggest a general pattern and expect, of course, that there are people who may not fit into these categories:

2.12.1 People with Low Scientific Rationality

The level of scientific rationality matters in rumors and gossip. In general, people with high scientific training and literacy are less inclined to engage in unverified information such as rumors and gossip. The saying goes: "Big minds talk about ideas but small minds talk about people" has a grain of truth. Why? Well, highly educated and rational people tend to be more critical, positivist or empirical in their thinking process because of the high level of scientific training. Thus, they tend not to be easily influenced and convinced by unverified information or stories with no scientific or solid evidence. Less educated people, of course, have their own rationality, but they tend to be less sophisticated and scientific in their thought processes and so can easily be influenced by rumors and gossip. Education is indeed power. It enlarges people's perspectives and makes people more rational and positivist in their thinking. Thus, they do not easily believe and pass unreliable information or news; unless, of course, they have hidden agenda to use rumors and gossip to achieve their own ends.

2.12.2 People with More Free Time

The volume of work and commitment can also affect people's capacity to create and/or circulate rumors and gossip. In general, busy people with serious commitments have less time for idle talks and thus may not generally engage in sharing or creating rumors and gossip. People with positions of authority with hectic schedule tend are not also inclined to engage in rumors and gossip, unless, of course, they can be used to advance their political career or vested interest. Moreover, career-oriented people and entrepreneurs with clear goals in professional and business life do not generally engage in idle talks and unproductive stories.

But people who are unemployed, retired or those with less work and daily appointment have more free time to engage in rumors and gossip. Rumors and gossip tend to fill up their idle time and make their minds active. This is particularly true to people who have peer groups. They are most likely to share idle talk, especially in a crowded neighborhood of informal settlers, for example. This can also be illustrated in one pre-school where the mothers and nannies were allowed to bring their kids to school and allowed inside the campus. While waiting for 2 hours daily, they developed close friendships and spent their idle time chatting and inventing and sharing rumors and gossip about what they observe and think about the school, teachers, and administrators. Rumors and gossip grow and travel faster among people who have less daily commitments and more time to spend for idle talk.

2.12.3 People Whose Dislike Patterns Support Rumors and Gossip

Creating and spreading rumor and gossip against a person or group have something to do with rumor-mongering or gossiper's moral life and patterns of dislike which s/he learned from his/her social upbringing and education. People who dislike the victim would most likely spread the rumors and gossip to discredit the person or group. Thus, if the recipient of the rumors are Republicans and involved the Democrats or vice-versa, they would more likely circulate the rumors because they support their dislikes against their political opponents. Just as students of a particular school who received a nasty rumor of a competitor school would more likely to circulate as it fits his/her hostile attitude towards it. On the internet, rumors and gossip are usually created and circulated by non-admirers and haters who dislike the victim. Death hoaxes of celebrities in the social media, for instance, are presumably not created by fans and admirers who wish all the best for their idols, but by haters who usually dislike either the talent, behavior or some personal traits of the celebrity. Justin Bieber, Adam Sandler, Aretha Franklin, Charlie Sheen, Bill Cosby, Lindsay Lohan, Nick Jonas and Taylor Swift are only some of the famous celebrities who are falsely reported to have died in popular social media sites.[42]

People, however, who received rumors or gossip that involve their own group, company or school, the reaction would be different. They are less likely to share them to others especially to those outside their own network. If rumor involves their company, for instance, they would more likely keep it to themselves. If they decide to share, it would more likely be confined only within their own trusted group or colleagues but not to unfriendly social networks, much more to their company's competitors. In other words, people would only circulate rumors and gossips if they support their cultural patterns of dislikes and protect or promote their personal or group interests. People would not circulate destructive rumors or gossips if they contradict their vested interests. Circulating nasty rumors and gossips that counter their vested interests would tantamount to self-crucifixion and thus less likely to happen. Thus, if employees or managers of Apple would less likely to spread nasty rumors that diminish the brand of their own company. If they do, it would probably be shared only within their own inner circles of friends and colleagues and not to competitors and hostile forces.

---

[42] Please see Lisa Mason, "Social Media Rumors and Hoaxes" at http://socialmediasun.com/social-media-rumors/.

2.12.4 People Living in Personalistic Environment

The social environment also matters in identifying the type of people who will spread rumors and gossip. The larger culture of society affects the cultural values of people in an organization. In a personalistic environment, what is more important are social ties rather than merit and qualification. Under this environment, people generally connect with their groups based on common interest and ties such as friendship, kinship or acquaintances in other organizations. In a personalistic organizational culture, small groups tend to compete strongly with other groups in an organization. To protect or promote the interest of one group over other competing groups, members oftentimes create or pass nasty rumors and gossip of members of other groups to maintain their dominance in the organization. Many Asian countries, especially in rural communities have this kind of social environment due to a strong kinship structure which basically connects people through social ties. It is not easy to change this type of environment in a short period of time. This related to the phase of urbanization and industrialization of a particular country. Thus, if people cannot withstand this type of system of the persistence of rumors and gossip, they transfer or migrate to another company or organization in highly rational and urbanized setting where merit and qualification counts rather than social ties.

2.13 Summary

This chapter has shown that rumors and gossip are stories, tales or news about a person or group which are presumed to be true but unverified. Rumors deal with issues that affect the common good while gossip deals with personal traits and characteristics that affect only particular individuals or groups. Rumors and gossip are inevitable in any social organization as people are social beings with different cultural training, taste, orientation to rules and social expectations. They change in content and evolved as they travel through time. Rumors and government are usually circulated by word-of-mouth in face-to-face interactions or through the internet and social media. Rumors and gossip continue to dominate society because they serve some important social functions. Rumors and gossip can be tools for publicity and popularity such as hyping of upcoming events such as new films. They can be warning signs that forewarn or prepare people and organizations of impending events such as a collapse of a business firm or job vacancy. And they can also be tools for domination and social resistance.

3 THE SOCIAL FUNCTIONS OF RUMORS AND GOSSIP

3.1 Introduction

This chapter discusses the nature and social functions of rumors and gossip in everyday life. Although they are generally seen as hearsay and are not acceptable in court proceedings, rumors and gossip nevertheless provide important functions in society that make life exciting, predictable, and meaningful to individuals and groups. This is why unverified stories such as rumors and gossip continue to influence people's daily life.

3.2 The Nature of Rumors and Gossip in Daily Life

Rumors and gossip are part of everyday life. People are social beings. They belong to the various social groups in society such as the family, team, peer, organization, neighborhood, or institution. And as social beings, they do not live isolated lives. They constantly mingle and interact with other people and groups in society whose vested interest, as well as social upbringing, cultural taste, level of education, and orientation to social norms and rules may be totally different from them. For this reason, disagreement, misinterpretation and conflict are inevitable in public life, both in the realm of face-to-face interaction and digital social exchange in the cyberspace.

Because of cultural diversity, people do not always agree on how they must appear, act, behave or communicate in public. Therefore, there are always people who cannot agree with others in public life. What they see or hear from others may sometimes conflict with their own set of adopted rules and social expectations. And when they cannot express their dislike or opposition directly to the person or party concerned in front of the person or group, they share it to others in digital and social media or by word-of-mouth in the form of a rumor or gossip, hoping that the person or party concerned can receive them indirectly and get the message.

Meanwhile, as the rumor or gossip travels through time from one person to another or from one social media user to another, the content tends to change depending on the interpretation and intention of the rumor monger or gossiper who shares it against the victim. Because of the social media, the content can easily be magnified and edited to make the rumor or gossip more palatable and attractive to internet users, especially if more people share similar hate patterns with those who created them. Thus, rumors and gossip evolve through time depending on the hate patterns of those who shared and interpreted them. A nasty rumor or post against President Obama who is a Democrat, for instance, is more likely to be magnified or shared by his political opponents--the Republicans, and not primarily by his fellow Democrats, political supporters and fans, although it's possible that there are Democrats who also hate him and join the rumor-mongering. Because rumors and gossip have no fixed content and solid empirical basis, they are therefore considered unreliable and hearsay in any court of law. Despite their unreliability and unacceptability in a court of law, rumors and gossip continue to exist in society because they perform some of the following social functions:

3.3.2 Informal Communication Channel

The release of official information in any social organization usually takes time because of the hierarchy of authorities who will approve it such the manager, division head, president, chairman of the board, etc. Moreover, an official memo or announcement represents a collective body such as the entire office, sub-unit, division, sister company, affiliate or the entire social organization itself. Therefore care is exercised in releasing official communication or information to the public. This makes official and formal information slow and thus allows people to speculate and search for answers of the current issue in advance. In this case, rumors and gossip serve as the fastest and easiest informal means to circulate information on the current issues of the social organization. Although unverified, rumors and gossip can provide advance information or clues of the things to come in an institution.

In one university, some rumors suggested that the president and vice-president will be replaced before the opening of a new school year. These rumors of a revamp turned out correct, but the names of candidates mentioned in the rumor were false. Thus, rumors and gossip may not be accurate, but they supply some advance information to people in an organization swiftly and provide them with some sense of control over an ambiguous situation.

3.3 Social Functions of Rumors and Gossip

3.3.1 Social Mechanism Discouraging Deviant Behavior

The threat of rumors and gossip can discourage people to break social norms or rules of society whether legal or moral. The thought of being caught, publicized and humiliated by the public if one is exposed doing illegal or immoral acts can be a sufficient psychological coercion that prevents people from committing rule-breaking behavior. Rumors and gossip are indicators of possible rule-breaking behaviors. They are like smoke that alerts people of a possible fire. Unless deliberately done and invented to destroy people, rumors and gossip would normally arise only if people or social organizations break some formal or informal societal norms or hide something fishy from the public. The KFC Restaurant's sale in China, for instance, plunged 37% the following month after rumors broke out and reported in state television that some poultry suppliers of KFC violated rules on drug use in chickens. There would not have rumors that lowered the sales of KFC if there was no probable violation of rules of it suppliers in the first place. The KFC is China's biggest restaurant chain, with more than 4,000 outlets and is planning to open 700 more branches.[43]

Rumors and gossip also discourage celebrities and public figures, being considered role models, to break legal or moral rules. When a person reaches the top and becomes rich and famous, many eyes are observing on him/her. Being a role model with millions of screaming fans, celebrities are expected to behave properly in private and public life, otherwise, people would create or spread all sorts of rumor and gossip to keep them adorable in the pedestal. Thus, Justin Bieber cannot be just live his life as he wants it to be. Being a celebrity and a role model for the youth, he has become a public property. Thus, people and his fans are closely observing his public life. The fast and viral rumors of his latest brushes with the law such as the rumors on drag racing or sleeping with a prostitute should be enough reminder for him to live an upright life as a public figure to avoid nasty intrigues and bad publicity which can lower his marketability as an artist. Rumors and gossip on teenage pregnancies of young actresses and celebrities also function as a social mechanism that discourages people to commit deviance. Despite their negative characteristics, rumors and gossip perform a positive social function of preventing and reminding people not to break the social norms and rules of society in order to avoid the psychological torture of being discovered and condemned by the public.

3.3.3 Entertainment, Energizer, and Source of Lessons

Despite their unreliability and unpredictability, rumors and gossip seem to be everywhere. "Gossip seeps through every school's halls, every bathroom's stall, and every city's malls. There's celebrity gossip, e-gossip, wrestling gossip, Hollywood gossip - even Barbie

---

[43] http://www.usatoday.com/story/money/business/2014/07/21/mcdonalds-kfc-china-scandal/12929885/.

gossip."⁴⁴ Rumors and gossip thrive in society because they amuse people and make them mentally charged—of course, momentarily and at the expense of the victim! So, one of the most popular uses of rumors and gossip in society is entertainment. This is one major reason people continue to patronize tabloids and gossip columns despite the unreliability of their news and stories. Practically all types of media have gossip columns to entertain people and fans of celebrities

Gossip is so popular in society and entertaining to many people of all walks of life that a whole industry is built around it, with millions of people patronizing it in various media. With the advent of the Internet and digital technology, gossip in the form of e-gossip has even reached unprecedented heights with some top most popular gossip websites dominating the industry.

Aside from entertainment, rumors and gossip can also jolt people from the boredom of routine and everyday life and charge the curiosity of their minds. How would you not react and listen if you hear a gossip the actor whom you admired as a fan for years as an epitome of manhood was rumored to be gay? Or you were informed of a blind item by a friend that the public official whom you have admired to be principled and honest for years has a viral video filming him caught in the act receiving bribe money, although it turned out to be a hoax? Rumors and gossip may turned out to be complete lies, but they activate people's mind by guessing or figuring out who the person is in the blind item, for instance. Rumors and gossip can therefore activate mind or distract it momentarily from its immediate concern or preoccupation. And some behavioral scientists theorize that the mind needs some distractions or variations in thought patterns once in a while to enhance the person's creativity and innovation.

Finally, rumors and gossip can provide some lessons of the ups and downs of life. No matter how incredible and ridiculous are their content, rumors and gossip make people reflect momentarily

---

⁴⁴ http://www.usatoday.com/story/money/business/2014/07/21/mcdonalds-kfc-china-scandal/12929885/.

somehow about their own life vis-à-vis the rumored story. Thus, when they hear rumors and gossip about tragedies, they would probably be grateful to God that this did not happen to them. In other words, rumors and gossip can also provide the recipient some insights on life's contingencies. Thus, if a person hears a story about a celebrity who became bankrupt after living a life of reckless spending and extravagance, s/he might probably learn about how to be wiser in spending money if s/he happens to be a extravagant person. Despite their negative label, rumors and gossip can also provide people some insights on the contingencies of life and some "reminders" of the possible consequences--as illustrated by the rumored story—if they live their life according to social norms and expectations.

3.3.4 Rumors and Gossip as Prediction

In some cases, rumors and gossip can be a prediction or anticipation of the future. They foretell the future. In one study by researchers at the University of Kentucky has found that office gossip isn't all bad. It was found out that latest rumors and gossip clue people in a company into things that are happening before they're officially announced, which can provide an edge in business dealings" Informal communication channels such as rumors and gossips tend to fast than formal announcements. Rumors and gossip prepare people of the opportunities to come. Thus, if one hears that someone in the company is about to be fired, probable candidates can prepare themselves in case they are called to justify why they deserved to be promoted to fill the vacant position.[45]

Some analysts believed that the bankruptcy of Lehman Brothers could have been prevented if its Wall Street bosses took the rumors seriously as predictions of the firm's impending demise and took some drastic and systemic actions, the crash probably be prevented. Rumors and speculations about the company's serious problems were already ripe months before the actual crash. People were talking about the failure of Lehman Brothers from the moment of the failure

---

[45] http://career-advice.monster.com/in-the-office/workplace-issues/good-office-gossip/article.aspx.

of Bear Stearns in March, or before, but Lehman bosses did not take the rumors as warning signs and address the problems squarely to prevent the collapse. Being optimistic views of its portfolio's worth, it ignored the rumors and theories that the US housing market had become dangerously overheated and that mortgage brokers were doling out loans to people who could never repay them [24]. As a result, Lehman Brothers filed bankruptcy protection on September 15, 2008, the largest bankruptcy filing in U.S. history [25].

Although rumors and gossip are generally unreliable, some may contain half-truths or may even turn out to be true especially the persistent ones. Rumors and gossip are not always totally surreal and unconnected to some factual reality. Some are connected somehow to the life of the victims. Practically, all organizations or business firms which became bankrupt are preceded forewarned by some stories of bankruptcy as illustrated in Lehman's case. Of course, there can be some fantastic stories or tales incorporated by people into their rumors or gossip, but there have to be indirect connections no matter how remote they can be; otherwise, people would take them as jokes and or not as serious rumors or gossip. Thus, if you create a gossip that Freddie Roach has just been hired as a coach in the NBA would be absurd and people would not take it seriously as a rumor or gossip as everybody knows that he is into boxing but not basketball. But if somebody creates a rumor that Pacquiao is drafted in the NBA with a very clever post, some people may bite it as credible. Many people, especially Filipinos, know that he has been in the professional basketball lately, being the playing coach of his own basketball team in the Philippine Basketball Association (PBA).

Creators of rumors and gossip usually find any form of weakness or rule-breaking behavior of their victim to create their intrigues and tales. Sarah Palin, for instance, became the target of more gossips by haters and critics because they also found some fault from her such as faking a pregnancy to protect her own daughter. Her family has problems with moral or legal norms.

But the more serious tales and allegations which look credible and believable; and palatable to public forums or social media, may contain some grain of truth. The person or group concerned must not therefore ignore or dismiss them immediately without first giving them some serious assessment what the rumor or gossip is all about and how and why they surface in public life. There is one theory which views rumors and gossip as warning signs to people or organizations of the some things to come as the saying goes: "If there's a smoke, there's fire!" Before Tim Cook publicly acknowledged that he is gay, gossip was said to have been circulating in Apple regarding his sexual orientation which eventually turned out to be true. Moreover, just before Enron was ordered closed by government regulators, for example, rumors already abound about the company's problems and yet these were not addressed to squarely to prevent the actual closure.

3.3.5 Tools for Publicity

Creating rumors and gossip can be deliberate act to gain publicity and popularity for people involved in an upcoming event or the event itself such as movie, concert, championship game, etc. This strategy is often used in the film entertainment industry. Handlers, talent managers or the producers with their networks in the broadcast and digital media would create gossip, for instance, about actress A having romantic date with the unexpected actor B before the release of a film in order to create buzz and generate publicity. Of course, the gossip is chosen and packaged by the producers and strategists of the movie to create a specific favorable effect and not just a reckless release of the lead actor or actress' life story and gossip which can destroy the overall hype and public expectation of the upcoming film. Some people think that bad publicity is still publicity. They don't care how bad is the news about them as long as they land on the front page.

There is a grain of truth to this. Bad publicity is publicity. In fact, bad publicity sells more that good publicity. The more deviant is the act or story such murdering a friend or boyfriend such in the case of Jodi Arias who was convicted of a first-degree murder for killing boyfriend Travis Alexander in June 2008 as well as former Patriot Stars Aaron Hernandez who was convicted of a first-degree murder for killing Odin Lloyd in June 2013. Both cases generated a lot of publicity and topped the headlines and posts for a longer period of time in broadcast, print, and social media. The gruesome details of these murders revealed during the trial and reported in the media have added even more attention to these cases. Publicizing heinous crimes or deviant acts can the fastest way to gain publicity, especially if done people of high social stature such as a celebrity politician or a business leader. The problem, however, of this kind of publicity is public acceptability. It does not create a good brand. The public does not generally want to associate with people with criminal background. So creating a rumor or gossip for publicity must be calibrated in such a way to achieve the intended goal. It must be connected with an organization or company's brand and image which is hyping the upcoming event, product, or service. It must not be overly negative that distracts from or destroy the overall objective of the campaign or hype.

3.3.6 Instruments for Domination

There are rumors and gossip which contain some serious accusation of rule-breaking and yet the victim can attest that it's totally false. This type of gossip is libelous with no solid factual basis and largely invented by a person or group who are out to ruin the reputation of others. This is particularly true in the cyberspace where there is anonymity and where networks are so closely-knit that a libelous post or video can go viral online with a mere touch or push of the share button. Celebrities can be more prone of this type of gossip than an unknown individual or group since they have wider publicity than ordinary people. Famous people have more materials in the digital media and cyberspace such as pictures, posts, tweets, and write-ups than ordinary people which can be used by haters to create and disseminate libelous tales and intrigues against them. With the advent of digital and nanotechnologies, there are now more techniques available on the Web which can be used by rumormongers and gossipers to destroy the honor of innocent people.

Rumors and gossip are not only warning signs, but tools for bullying by those who want control and humiliate innocent but popular individuals. One classic example of this type of destructive gossip was the case of the High School teacher and Cincinnati

Bengals NFL cheerleader Sarah Jones. Sarah Jones life and career was all full of roses until a series of destructive gossip posted in blogs accusing her of sleeping with numerous people including a 17-year-old student; thus, she was nicknamed in the online gossip as the "female [Jerry] Sandusky," linking her to the former Penn State assistant football coach who was convicted of sexually assaulting 10 boys.[46]

3.3.7 Tools for Bullying

Bullying through the use of rumors and gossip is a form of controlling and dominating others in real life or on the internet. Whether in the classroom, office, locker rooms, or cyberspace, bullies dominate their victims by creating and circulating nasty stories ridicule or dishonor against them. This is a form of psychological conditioning by bullies to further weaken the victims' capacity to resist. Bullying can even be more vicious on the internet. Because of anonymity in the cyberspace, the victims may not be aware at first that there were already online gossips circulating around by bullies and if they discover it, it is already too late as the malicious rumors and gossip may have probably been circulated in the cyberspace

Rachael Neblett, a seventeen-year-old high school student from Kentucky, for instance, began receiving threatening emails through her MySpace account, in the summer of 2006 before committing suicide. The anonymous emails were said to be a stalking terroristic nature which tortured her psychologically.[47]

Bullying using the cyberspace and electronic technology is popularly called cyberbullying. Humiliating the weak using the digital and electronic media includes "mean text messages or emails, rumors sent by email or posted on social networking sites, and embarrassing pictures, videos, websites, or fake profiles."[48]

---

[46] http://www.huffingtonpost.com/2012/08/01/former-cheerleader-sarah-jones-bengals-female- sandusky_n_1727967.html.
[47] http://www.puresight.com/Real-Life-Stories/rachael-neblett.html.

[48] http://www.stopbullying.gov/cyberbullying/index.html.

Bullies can manufacture stories, false accusations or even true stories to put the victims in a bad light in order to humiliate and symbolically take control their weak and defenseless victims in real and digital life. The cyberbully can be intense which can lead to suicide of the victims. Hannah Smith, a 14-year old girl from Leicestershire, England, for instance, hanged herself in her bedroom following taunts on the Ask.fm social networking site, a question-and-answer social networking site that allows anonymous participation. Bullies on Ask.fm urged her to drink bleach and cut herself. After her death, Hannah's father found a note that read:

"As I sit here day by day I wonder if it's going to get better. I want to die, I want to be free. I can't live like this anymore. I'm not happy."[49]

Ryan Halligan, a 13-year old student from Vermont, killed himself after he was ridiculed and humiliated by peers at school and on-line. In particular, he committed suicide after being gossiped as a gay by bullies in AOL IM account.[50]

Rumors and gossip used for cyberbulling can also be based on facts or real conversation and recording which are shameful if divulged publicly. "Daniel Perry, 17, for instance, was believed to be simply chatting over webcam with a girl when blackmailers jumped into the Skype chat and told him that he'd "better off dead" if he would not pay them up because they would share a recording of the conversation. Terrified, Perry, within an hour of the threat, jumped from a bridge near his home and died.

"Indeed, Perry's death is only the latest in a troubling trend in which teens feel suicide is their only option in the face of Internet shaming. Tormentors often trick children into posing naked or

---

[49] http://www.puresight.com/Real-Life-Stories/hannah-smith.html.

[50] http://www.puresight.com/Real-Life-Stories/ryan-halligan-1989-2003.html.

carrying out sex acts on webcams. They bully their victims into paying up or sending further compromising images if they don't want family, friends, and classmates to know."[51]

3.3.8 Tools for Politics

Rumors and gossip are used only to control and dominate the weak but also to control resources and power in a social organization. Internal politics and group bullying are inevitable in school, business firm or any social organization. Politics is everywhere, especially in a social organization which has a weak social control and law enforcement and where social connections or ties are more important than merits and qualifications. Politics has been classically defined as "who gets what, when and how". This means that access to resources in society would depend largely on the social standing and power of the person or group requesting. If the group or person requesting is powerful and has connections, s/he can easily receive what s/he wants in a shorter period (when) and in a most convenient way (how). But if the group or person has less power and connection, s/he usually receives what s/he requested in a longer period if not disapproved and in a most inconvenient way. Kerkvliet (1995) defined politics broadly as comprising "the activities in which people, groups, and organizations engage in order to control, allocate, and use resources; politics also includes the values and ideas underlying those activities.[52]

In any human organization, whether in school or business firm, there is always a dominant group which tries to control resources and power. The sociologist C. Wright Mills (1956) calls this group as the power elite or a relatively small, loosely knit group of people who tend to dominate policy making in an organization.[53] In a social

---

[51] http://dailydot117.rssing.com/chan-12234288/all_p2.html.
[52] Kervliet, B. (1995). The Power of Everyday Politics: How Vietnamese Peasants Transformed national Policy. Ithaca, NY: Cornell University Press.

[53] Mills, C.W. (1956). *The Power Elite*. Oxford, UK: Oxford University Press.

organization such as a business firm, the power elite is an informal group whose opinions affect policy making and daily politics inside the organization. The members may be of similar positions such a group of managers or a mixture of people in a company which come from different division and position but bonded by a common interest and social ties. The leader of this group usually has powerful backers or connections with the owners or top executives of the business firms or top administrators in a school setting. In a classroom, the power elite can be a group of students who are "favorites" of the teacher or class adviser.

One powerful tool which the power elite can use to control politics and put down any perceived competitor or threat to their position are rumors and gossips. Since this group has powerful connections and regular contacts with the top management, the members can easily circulate rumors and gossips against their perceived or real competing groups try to challenge their established position in the organization. Thus, if there is a vacancy in a business firm for a management position and one member of the power elite is a contender against another applicant who comes from another group in a company, the power elite may sow intrigues and gossip against the other applicant in order to ensure that their co-member can get the position.

3.3.9 "Weapons of the Weak" for Resistance

It is a common pattern that people who occupy a public position and abuse their power and authority would always invite social resistance from their constituents. The prudent use of authority is important to avoid resistance from subordinates.

Sowing rumor and gossip can be used by the strong to bully and control the weak. But they can also be used by the weak to fight back in a subtle way. Some contemporary theories in the social sciences view power in the continuum and exercised in ordinary places such as the home, classroom, or office. At one end is complete domination and control of the strong and powerful over the weak such as a very authoritarian and abusive boss over his employees, but at the other end is social resistance, both active and passive, such as employees sowing intrigues and gossip against the authoritarian boss without his knowledge. An employee can fight back secretly against her authoritarian boss by spreading gossip about his/her sexual orientation, appearance, character and any negative trait to his/her trusted friends and colleagues in the company in order to put him/her in bad light indirectly or covertly. By doing this, the employees would be able to get back at his/her boss symbolically and release some of her pent-up energies or anger.

Rumors and gossip, therefore, also perform the important positive function of neutralizing bullying and discouraging anti-social behavior. A Stanford University research confirmed the positive function of rumors and gossip to group harmony. It showed that gossip and talking about people behind their backs, despite their negative connotation, can actually enhance group cooperation and discourage anti-social behavior. It indicated that gossip and ostracism can be used as tools by which groups reform bullies, thwart exploitation of "nice people" and encourage group harmony.[54]

Social resistance through gossip can also happen between students and their "abusive" or overtly strict professors or between any two parties where one group is dominated by another group. The weak often fights back indirectly and covertly since they are powerless to confront the strong openly. Sowing rumors and gossip against the powerful is a passive or covert form of social resistance. Rumors and gossip can be considered what James Scott (1986) calls as "weapons of the weak."[55] A social resistance can be overt, such as verbal retaliation, petition letter, protest, or outright disobedience. But it can also be passive such as intentionally underperforming one's task to embarrass the manager to higher authorities or sowing intrigues, rumors, and gossip at the back of the boss, administrator, teacher, coach, or manager. Although covert and appear insignificant,

---

[54] http://news.stanford.edu/news/2014/january/upside-of-gossip-012714.html.
[55] Scott, J.C. (1986). Weapons of the Weak: *Weapons of the weak: everyday forms of peasant resistance.* New Haven and London: Yale University Press.

rumors and gossip can be effective tools to neutralize the domination of the bully, powerful and abusive.

3.4 Summary

This chapter briefly discussed the significance of rumors and gossip in daily life. Unverified stories continue to exist in society because they perform significant social functions. Rumors and gossip are informal channels of communication that prepare people of the future. They can also inhibit people to break the formal and informal norms in society as well as entertain, energize, and provide them with some life lessons. Lastly, rumors and gossip can become tools for publicity, domination, bullying, politics, and social resistance.

4 BREEDING GROUND OF RUMORS AND GOSSIP

4.1 Introduction

This chapter identifies the common breeding ground for rumors and gossip. Although they can be found in almost all cultures and places, rumors and gossip can prevalent to certain type of people and situations. It introduces the reader to the most places, situations and social organizations in which unverified information and stories can most likely thrive. Not all social situations are prone to rumors or gossip. It depends on the social structure of organizations, institutions, and societies. Information management, power structure, and law enforcement in a given social system play an important role in the production and distribution of rumors and gossip.

4.2 Organizational Factors Affecting Rumors and Gossip

The persistence of rumors and gossip does not only depend on the self-discipline and moral character of individuals who circulate them, but also on the type of social environment and structure. The interaction between people and social structure is dialectic. The individual affects the social structure and the social structure influences the individuals. If the social structure is lax in controlling the behavior of individuals within the social organization, rumors and gossip would most likely thrive. But if the structure is transparent and efficient in law enforcement, rumors and gossip would less likely grow. The degree of social control and the type of corporate culture of an organization are two important social factors that determine the existence and persistence of rumors and gossip.

4.2.1 The Degree of Social Control

"In the most fundamental terms, "social control" referred to the capacity of a society to regulate itself according to desired principles and values. Sociological analysis has the task of exploring the conditions and variables likely to make this goal attainable."[56] Critical theory classifies social control of people's behavior into two: interior and external control. The internal control is what people commonly called as self-disciple while the external refers to the law enforcement system in the social environment such CCTV camera or other monitoring devices or law enforcers such as government agents, police, principal, checker, security guards, etc. who monitor a rule-breaking behavior of people. External discipline is taught and learned at home, in school or one's culture. The Japanese, for instance, have a strong sense of honesty taught by their culture. So, they do not need, in general, to be watched all the time to avoid rule-breaking behaviors. Spreading rumors and gossip is one of the rule-breaking behaviors. Although all people rumor and gossip, the intensity of this act, however, differs from one social organization to another. We can notice that in a very rational, efficient and orderly system, there is less rumors and gossip whereas in a very personalistic system where the rules are lax and system seems to only some groups in an organization, rumors and gossip abound. But a rational system such as McDonald's or other fast-food chain setup, everybody knows exactly what to do in the workplace since the system is so well-organized and transparent. In this case, the degree of rationality,

---

[56] Janowitz, M. (1975). Sociological Theory and Social Control. *American Journal of Sociology,* Vol.. 81, No. 1 (Jul., 1975), pp. 82.

efficiency and transparency is important in the external environment to avoid any rule-breaking behavior such rumors and gossip. The use of technologies to guide behavior can also minimize ambiguous situations which can lead to rumors and gossip.

4.2.2 The Size and Level of Efficiency and Rationality

The prevalence of rumors and gossip is somehow related to the size, efficiency and level of complexity of a social organization. In a large business firm such a multinational corporation, the business operation is highly impersonal, efficient, rational and predictable due to the use of technology, rumors and gossip are minimal. Thus, rumors and gossip tend to be low. But in smaller firms where face-to-face interactions are high and rules are often negotiated, rumors and gossip tend to be prevalent. A family business with fewer employees can be personalistic in interactions and thus prone to rumors and gossips especially if the company rules are lax.

Size also affects the level of rumors and gossip circulating in a particular school. A small community college, for instance, where population is low and students and teachers interact more often personally is more prone to rumors and gossip than a big university with a high population and level of anonymity. Rumors and gossip in large universities tend to be more limited in a particular department or group where there is a high level of acquaintance. Of course, if the rumors and gossip's content affects the entire school or university, the circulation and exchange would spread throughout the entire institution and beyond. So, the size of a school, business firm or social organization, aside from other factors, matters if one plans to enroll or apply for a job to a particular school or company.

4.2.3 The Level of Discontent

Aside from the size and level of efficiency and rationality, the level of contentment of people in an organization also determines the volume and persistence of rumors and gossip. If people in an organization such as students and administrators in school or employees and managers in a business firm are discontented with any policy or procedure and no satisfactory actions are done by top managers to address them, then rumors and gossip would more likely thrive in the organization. Thus, an important indicator of the prevalence of rumors and gossip of a particular company or institution is the level of discontent of people inside the organization. If there is labor unrest inside the company, for instance, then those who want to join the firm would must lots of rumors and gossip circulating in the workplace. Knowing the level of discontent in a social organization is difficult to discover especially for people are still planning to join the organization or they have not done an informal background investigation of the firm's organizational culture. In most cases, new recruits normally do not stay in a business firm if they discover that rumors and gossip hinder their professional growth. Students who are transferees from other schools would not also survive in the new school if parents would not do a background check of the new school's culture with regard to rumors and gossip. In basic education, rumors and gossip are often used by bullies to humiliate the weak and neophyte students.

4.2.4 The Type of Organizational Culture

The magnitude of rumors and gossip in an organization would depend largely on its organizational culture and the overall social environment. If you have an environment which is efficient, transparent, supportive and rewarding, one cannot expect much rumors and gossip against the school or company would thrive. Expect this type of school to attract instead the best students or company to attract the best and most qualified talents (Is Google of this kind? That's why job hunters prefer to join this company?). Thus, Richard Branson's advice with regard to hiring people into the company is wise. He said that the foremost consideration in hiring people into the firm is to determine whether the applicant's personality can fit into the company's culture.[57] An applicant may be highly qualified for the job. But if his/her personality does not fit into the firm's culture, s/he will not last in the job. Thus, recruiters

---

[57] Branson, R. (2013). How I Hire: Focus on Personality. September 13,2013.https://www.linkedin.com/pulse/20130923230007-204068115-how-i-hire-focus-on-personality/.

and HR personnel must have a firm grasp of their company's organizational culture to be able to select the most qualified and culturally fit applicant for the firm. A highly qualified new employee who is not used to rumors and gossips would surely leave the company after a brief stint in the workplace or a highly academic student to transfer to another school. Career or success-oriented people do not usually like a social environment that is prone with rumors and gossip. It distracts them from their long-term goals in life.

An organizational culture is a lived experience. Its totality could not be described on paper since it is the entire way of life of a particular business organization. It can only be fully understood and felt by people if they are immersed in it, participating in its day-today activities for a considerable period of time. Once people become regular members of an organization as students, employees or managers and actively interacting with people, structures, and rules, they would soon discover its basic cultural patterns. Thus, a new employee in a company or student in a school cannot immediately be familiar with the culture or way of life of the new organization. S/he cannot immediately know the "rumor and gossip" practices of the place. It takes some time before s/he knows whether the entire organization is prone to idle talk or not.

4.2.5 The Level of Cultural "Toxicity"

One sure breeding ground for rumor and gossip is a social system or a company with a "toxic" organizational culture. The term "toxic" culture is not used in the social sciences since it implies a value-judgment. But this is popular in the business industry. A "toxic" culture manifest inequality within a particular organization or institution. It usually favors one group or network of groups over other leading to distortion of information and favoritism in the sharing of resources inside the company or organization. In her article, "7 Signs You're working in a Toxic Workplace," Bruna Matinuzzi (2013) identified important signs of a toxic company culture which is worth citing here:[58]

---

[58] Martinuzzi, Bruna (2013). "7 signs You're Working in A Toxic Office".https://www.americanexpress.com/us/small-

4.2.5.1 Lack of Equality

In a toxic culture, there is a double standard in the application of rules: one of those who are close with power holders and another for those who are powerless or those who have weak corporate connections. Power cliques are usually given a preferential treatment with regard to the enforcement of company rules in a toxic environment.

4.2.5.2 Thriving Deviant Cliques

A band of employees can form a negative clique whose members behave like corporate teenagers. They put a negative spin on most company initiatives covertly.

4.2.5.3 Malice Trumping Kindness

"Bad" people in the company do their greatest damage by sabotaging anything that honest and good employees are trying to accomplish for the good of the business organization. They continuously create roadblocks to sabotage sincere efforts of some employees to help improve the company.

4.2.5.4 Managers Playing Favorites

The manager spends more face time with a selected few than with others. The favorites are publicly praised by the manager for their work, while those who are not mentioned end up feeling bad.

4.2.5.5 Hiring of Unqualified Cronies

Power cliques of employees and managers in the company

---

business/openforum/articles/7-signs-youre-working-in-a-toxicoffice/.

lobby senior executives to hire friends who are clearly not a good fit for the job or the culture. They bypass the normal recruitment processes to enlist more cronies in their negative camp.The result: the company hires incompetent employees who are not loyal to the institution but the sponsoring power clique.

4.2.5.6 The Poster Boy

This is an individual who is the antithesis of what a leader should be. He is looking out for number one—his prime motivation is the pursuit of power and money. He is untrustworthy, cheats his partners and every other stakeholder, flirts with female staff, and gossips about one team member to another.

4.2.5.7 "Lucrezia Borgia is on Staff"

Lucrezia Borgia is a metaphor for the bright, clever and evil employee "behind the throne" who drives many good people away from the company. In the eyes of management, this employee is considered a trusted and company cop who allegedly has the company's best interest at heart. She has the ear of upper management who are oblivious to the harm she is causing and believe all the filtered information they receive from her. In a business, there are always senior employees who pretend to protect the company's interest when, in fact, they are only promoting their own vested interests![59]

4.2.6 The Efficient and "Happy" Organizational Culture

In an organizational culture where politics is less and "everyone is happy", it is unlikely to see employees leaving or maligning their managers through rumors and gossip. If there is a high level of job satisfaction and compensation, efficient and clear information system, and strong corporate bonding, one can expect fewer rumors and

---

[59] Ibid.

gossip. But if the company's system is irrational, unpredictable, full of power cliques, and low in compensation and rewards, expect higher levels of rumors and gossip from people who want to control the firm's resources and rewards. Rumors and gossip are instruments of power and resistance. Any power holder or resister in the company can use them to advance his/her personal and group interests. Resisters manufacture information or even use negative facts and shocking discoveries to change the system and weaken their enemies in the business firm. Thus, a company may seem functional outwardly, but crumbling due to internal dissatisfaction, division, and power struggle of employees and managers to control the system inwardly. Because of this internal dissension, the company's productivity suffers and the personnel's creativity is stifled. Under a "bad" system, people's energies are more spent in politics than promoting innovation and achieving the firm's goals and forecasts.

4.3 Rumors and Gossip and Ambiguous Situations

Rumors and gossip thrive in ambiguous and doubtful situations. They remind people, especially public figures, to follow the social norms, whether moral or legal. They also prepare and warn people to cope with an impending corporate change. If a business firm, for instance, is about to collapse, rumors and gossip would usually precede it to prepare employees and managers of its actual demise and to enable them to prepare psychologically and to start searching for new jobs promptly. If not handled properly, rumors and gossip can wreck careers, sabotage ambitions or even topple big companies. With the advent of the internet and digital technology, rumors and gossip can spread like forest fires, ready to destroy people and companies. Indeed, rumors and gossip are unavoidable in corporate and public life. One cannot avoid rumors and gossip, especially if one lives in a corporate culture where "playing politics" is a dominant mode of interaction. What is important then is how one handles them and turn them into challenges and motivations for growth.

4.3.1 News Blackout or Lack of Information

Information dissemination and management is crucial in avoiding or minimizing rumors and gossip. The most common cause of an ambiguous situation which can lead to rumors and gossip is the absence or lack of clear and credible information on current issues that affect a social organization. Normally, a transparent situation where people in a given organization whether in school, workplace or institution knows what is happening around them does not generate a question, doubt and discontent which lead to rumors and gossip. Rumors and gossip can be minimized in a workplace, for instance, where any significant change of position, schedule or task is posted promptly either through online or written communication posted in a bulletin board visible to all with mobile or telephone numbers where questions or clarifications of employees can be answered by the manager. But in office where the communication process is controlled by the authoritarian manager and divulge only news and changes in the company even ordinary matters only if s/he sees fit and only to some trusted subordinates within the office, then gaps of information and delays of its release can generate rumors and gossip. Lack of information often generates curiosity in people which can result in speculations, fictitious stories and intrigues to fill-up the gap.

4.3.2 Lack of Credibility of the Information

The available and frequent information may not be sufficient in some cases especially where there mismanagement in a given organization. No amount of information from the management can quell rumors and gossip if the information is unconvincing to the people concerned. Employees may not bite the explanation of the management over some issues if the content is manifestly unconvincing and especially if given through spokesperson who cannot directly answer questions from the discontented in a group meeting, for instance. This can even given an impression that the management is hiding something and can further intensify the rumors. In short, the quality of information, and not just frequency, matters to minimize rumors and gossip. With regard to gossip which is connected to the personal traits, it is the decision of the person concerned whether to tell the truth or not. But if s/he wants to avoid the recurring gossip or issue against him/her such as sexual orientation, finding another social environment can be an option to gain peace of mind if s/he is not yet ready to go out, otherwise s/he has to devise creative ways to overcome this to remain in the social organization such as trying to be helpful to people around him/her. People do not generally hurt their benefactors or those who are friendly and generous to them. They can easily disregard their "deviant" personal traits of people who can empathize with them.

4.4 Summary

This chapter has discussed the breeding ground for rumors and gossip. Unverified information does not just thrive everywhere. It depends on the social structure and culture of the organization and society. Companies with level of "toxicity" in their corporate culture tend to be prone to rumors and gossip. Moreover, the existence of deviant cliques or power elites as well as lack of clear and convincing information in the workplace and business organizations can also intensify rumors and gossip.

5 DISTINGUISHING THE TRUTH FROM LIES, RUMORS, AND GOSSIP

5.1. Introduction

It is not totally impossible to determine whether the speaker who shares a story or news is telling the truth or inventing and spreading rumors, gossip and lies. To know whether the speaker is telling the truth or lies and half-truths such as rumors and gossip, this chapter guides people who receive unverified information on how to observe the speaker's behavior, analyze the content, and understand the meaning of storyteller's body language or symbolic gestures.

5.2 How to Judge the Truthfulness of Information

5.2.1 Judge the Face Value of the Story or Information

Is the story or information easily believable?

One important way to know whether the story or information is the truth or a mere rumor or gossip is to examine its face value or inner consistency. There are some stories and information which can easily identified as mere urban legend, rumor or gossip by just examining the story or news itself to know whether it truthful or unreliable.

5.1.2 Examine the Internal Validity

Are the elements of the story or information internally logical, consistent and human possible?

If one cannot ascertain whether the story is a rumor, gossip or the truth by judging the face value of the story or information, the recipient must proceed to the next method of verification—analyzing the logic and internal consistency of the story or information. If one or more elements of the story are contradictory, humanly impossible or incredible, then the recipient can assume that the story is a hoax, rumor or gossip.

5.1.3 Test the Credibility of the Storyteller

Is the storyteller credible?

The most convenient and obvious way to determine whether the speaker is telling the truth or just spreading rumors or gossips is to test the credibility of the speaker. If the recipient personally knows the speaker for a long time, s/he has more or less has a general idea of the credibility and integrity of the speaker, whether s/he is an honest person and who has always been speaking the truth in the past. The test of credibility and honesty of the speaker is even more imperative if the nature of the story or information is serious or if the speaker testified that s/he has a personal knowledge of the story or an eyewitness of the event such as sharing a story that s/he saw his boss having an extramarital affairs with an office mates by seeing him having a date with her in a restaurant.

The power and authority of the speaker can also generally indicate whether the speaker is credible or not, assuming, of course, that s/he is not intentionally hiding something. Thus, a manager who shares an information or theory about the possible cause of the company's financial loss can be more credible than a rank-and-file employee who is not in a better position to understand the internal management problem of the firm. A lawyer as well as a witness who share their personal experience of corruption in courts can be more credible than a non-lawyer who is unfamiliar with the judicial system.

5.1.4 Judge the Storyteller's Body Language

Does the speaker's body language indicate lying?

If the storyteller or gossiper is a total stranger to the recipient of the unverified information and there is way to double-check the veracity of information as such calling a colleague or trusted friend, then there is no other reliable way to check the veracity of the information but to look into the speaker's body language or symbolic gestures during the conversation to search for clues of his/her honesty and sincerity.

Observing the body language of the person who shares an unverified story or information can be a smart way to test whether the speaker is telling a truth or a lie. Understanding the meaning of the speaker's facial expressions and symbolic gestures during the conversation can provide a better picture whether the story or information is accurate or simply a rumor or gossip. Social scientists, particularly psychologists. have developed some sort of criteria and classification of actions and symbolic gestures, based on scientific research studies which suggest whether a person is lying or not. The first step is to know whether what the speaker is passing on a false or a true. By asking questions and observing the person's reaction and body language during the personal encounter, the recipient can gauge if the storyteller is honest.

If the recipient is holistic in his/her observation techniques, s/he must not only be contented with what s/he sees or hears during the conversation but must also look for clues and inconsistencies in words and symbolic gestures. In this case, s/he must know how to interpret the meaning of what the speaker says and what his/her body language conveys during the conversation.

Below are some common behavioral indicators or signs observed by experts as indicators of lying. These can be used as well as a guide to search for clues whether the gossiper is spreading the truth or simply lying and passing a rumor or gossip. The recipient, of course, must not use these indicators as absolutes. Prudence must be exercised in applying them to concrete situations, especially outside the American cultural setting. If the speaker is a foreigner and has a different set of gestures of lying, the recipient must first suspend his/her judgment and does some cross-cultural research after the conversation to know the speaker's expressions of lying. The use of other techniques to validate initial assessment during this encounter is highly recommended in order to avoid misjudgment. Here are some common signs indicating that a person is probably lying (Glass, 2013):[60]

5.1.4.1 Avoiding Eye Contact

The storyteller asserts that s/he is telling the truth but avoids eye contact can indicate that s/he is probably telling a lie. Avoiding eye contact when confronted about an information is a sign that his/her story maybe unreliable. Avoiding eye contact usually arouses suspicion that the person is not honest with his/her words. Moreover, lack of eye contact may indicate that storyteller lacks self-confidence, thus suggesting that s/he is not sure with the veracity with what s/he is sharing.

5.1.4.2 Changing Head Position Quickly

The storyteller may be lying or hiding something to the recipient if s/he suddenly makes a head movement when asked with a direct question. If s/he retracts, jerks back, bows down, cocks, or tilts his/her head to the side before responding to a question can indicate lying or mentally reserving something untruthful.

---

[60]Glass, L. (2013). *The Body Language of Liars: From Little White Lies to Pathological Deception—How to See through the Fibs, Frauds, and Falsehoods People Tell You Every Day.* Franklin Lakes, SJ: Career Press.

5.1.4.3 Changing Breathing Pattern Fast

The recipient can easily feel if the front in front of him/her changes breathing pattern fast. This change of breathing pattern is said to be a reflex action for someone who is hiding something. If the rumor monger's breathing changes, his/her shoulders will rise and his/her voice can get shallow, then s/he is probably bluffing. S/he is out of breath because his/her heart rate and blood flow change. These types of changes are usually attributed to someone who is nervous and feeling tense because of lying.

5.1.4.4 Standing Still

It's common to see people to fidget when they get nervous. But it is also possible that they do not move at all when they are nervous because of lying. "This may be a sign of the primitive neurological 'fight,' rather than the 'flight,' response, as the body positions and readies itself for possible confrontation. "When you speak and engage in normal conversation, it is natural to move your body around in subtle, relaxed, and, for the most part, unconscious movements. So if you observe a rigid, catatonic stance devoid of movement, it is often a huge warning sign that something is off."

5.1.4.5 Repeating Words or Phrases

The speaker is trying to convince the recipient by repeating himself/herself of something, then s/he is probably lying. In this case, s/he is trying to validate the lie in his/her mind. S/he may say: "I didn't...I didn't..." over and over again. The repetition is also a way to buy themselves time as they attempt to gather his/her thoughts.

5.1.4.6 Providing Too Much Information

When someone goes on and on and gives you too much information — information that is not requested and especially an excess of details — there is a very high probability that the speaker may not be telling the truth. "Liars often talk a lot because they are hoping that, with all their talking and seeming openness, others will believe them."

5.1.4.7 Touching or Covering the Mouth

It is also a sign of lying if the gossiper will automatically put his/her hands over his/her mouth when s/he doesn't want to deal with an issue or answer a question. This can mean that s/he is not revealing everything or s/he just don't want to tell the truth.

5.1.4.8 Covering Instinctively Vulnerable Body Part

Instinctively covering vulnerable parts such as the throat, chest, head, or abdomen when asked a question can also be a sign that the speaker is caught off-guarded and thus a sign that s/he is hiding something.

5.1.4.9 Shuffling of Feet

If the storyteller is in a sitting position, shuffling his/her feet during conversation can indicate that s/he is uneasy and nervous of something and thus probably hiding something to the recipient. It can also indicate that s/he wants to leave the situation or want to walk away to avoid embarrassment because his/her story is a rumor or a gossip with no hard facts to support them. His/her body would show if s/he is comfortable of telling the truth or nervous of hiding something during the conversation.

5.1.4.9.10 Difficulty in Speaking

Liars can run out of words or show difficulty in speaking to defend his/her lies. This is caused by the decrease of salivary flow in the nervous system during times of stress which can dry out the mucous membranes of the mouth. But the recipient should also be alert to sudden lip biting or pursed lips by the gossiper as a potential sign of lying.

5.1.4.9.11 Staring Without or Too Much Blinking

People who lie usually break their eye contract with others. But it is also possible that they go the extra mile to maintain eye contact in attempt to control and manipulate others. Unusual staring without blinking at regular intervals by the interviewee can indicate lying. Honest people will occasionally shift their eyes around and may even look away from time to time when explaining something. Liars, on the other hand, will use a cold, steady gaze to intimidate and control others. But the recipient should also watch out for rapid blinking which can also indicate that the speaker is lying.

5.1.4.9.12 Pointing a Lot

When a liar becomes hostile or defensive, s/he is attempting to turn the tables on the other person. The liar can get hostile during the conversation if the recipient has discovered his/her lies, which may result in a lot of pointing. In this case, the gossiper or rumor monger is showing his/her true colors.

5.1.49.13 Rubbing or Touching the Nose

Finally, if the speaker touches or rubs his/her nose before answering a direct question, the recipient must be alert of lying. Rubbing or touching one's nose in an interrogation is generally considered a sign that the person is hiding something.

5.3 Cultural Differences in Verifying Lying

There are cultural differences in how individuals explain their lying and truth-telling tendencies.[61] What constitutes lying, for instance, in one country or region may not be lying in other parts of the world. But telling the truth is not always the most important consideration particularly in Asian culture especially if it conflicts with other higher cultural values such communal honor or harmony. Japan has one of the most underdeveloped legal systems in the world because the Japanese prefer a peaceful amicable settlement of legal cases rather than engaging in the Western-inspired court room drama

---

[61] Choi, H. J.,Park, H.S., & Oh, J.Y.(2011). Cultural differences in how individuals explain their lying and truth-telling tendencies.*International Journal of Intercultural Relations,* 35 (6): 749-766.

which conflicts with their cultural value of communal harmony. Vietnamese would also avoid public confrontation and show their disapproval in public. They even put a smile even if they disagree with someone in a conversation. They don't usually show it in their word or face. For the West, this can be considered lying as the external behavior does not indicate what is in the mind of the speaker. For Filipinos, when reject an invitation, they don't directly tell the inviting party with a blunt embarrassing "No" but indirectly using euphemistic language such "Let me see" in order not to hurt the feelings of the person inviting. The anthropologist Frank. Lynch, S.J. (1973) calls this as Smooth Interpersonal Relationship (SIR) of the Filipinos which implies giving more importance to harmony in one's group and to avoid hurting others' feelings.[62]

In sum, it is important to know the cultural training of the storyteller when assessing body language and verifying the honesty of the speaker. People from the East have different attitudes and expressions of lying. Unlike Americans and Europeans, Asians generally do not appreciate people who are "brutally honest" or who want to get to the point quickly. Unlike the Western culture, the number one cultural consideration in Asia, particularly Southeast Asia, is to save one's face in public and not to lose one's cool in conversation. Shouting or arguing in public is strictly frowned upon; causing a scene actually makes bystanders to lose face through embarrassment. Although frustrating, keeping one's cool calm until both parties have reached a resolution is for Asians. The expression of lying, rumor, and gossip vary across different cultures in the world. To know the truth requires anthropological knowledge of culture.

5.4 Summary

This chapter discussed some tips on how to distinguish the truth from lies, rumors and gossip. To know the veracity of stories, one

---

[62] Lynch, F. (1973) Social acceptance, reconsidered. In Frank Lynch and Alfonso de Guzman II (eds.), Four Readings on Philippine Values (IPC Papers No.2). Quezon.

must test the credibility of the speaker as well as the internal validity of the story and the body language of the speaker whether he or she was lying. Some body movements can provide one a clue concerning the intention of the storyteller and truthfulness of his/her story. The movements of the speaker's eyes, hands, feet, head, etc. can tell a lot to the listener whether he or she is lying or bluffing.

6 COMPANY RUMORS

6.1 Introduction

This chapter explains the nature of company and commercial rumors and how to address them in the business organization, workplace, and market. It provides some recommendations on how to counteract malicious rumors that tend to weaken the business organization. When rumors become more destructive in the workplace, it suggests some legal actions victims can file in court to altogether stop the malicious rumors.

6.2 Nature of Company Rumors

Rumors are not only limited to in ordinary life but also in companies, large or small, whether public, private, not for profit or governmental. False rumors are typically the consequence of two unrelated problems: poor communication between upper management and employees (regardless whether they are technical or administrative staff or lower-level management) and an inherent desire in some individuals to be thought of as having access to inside information.[63]

---

[63] Voas, J. M. (2002). Corporate rumors and conspiracy theories. *IT*

False rumors can originate from any source. But in a company, Voas (2002) suggested that rumors usually originate from nonmanagement employees and more specifically by junior-level employees (such those fresh from out of college). One of the main reasons is that they possess the least access to senior staff meetings and corporate books and thus leaves them with little information about discussions behind closed doors. But colleagues at other companies also tell stories of very mean-spirited rumors.[64]

When understood and controlled, the office grapevine can serve as a legitimate form of communication. However, when it is uncontrolled, rumor-based talk presents a potential danger. Rumors tend to increase during times of stress.[65] (Hunter, 1983). Rumors during retrenchment abound too and : 1.structure and reduce anxiety, 2. make sense of the situation, 3. organize strategic posture, and 4. signal status or power.[66]

Workplace rumors are systematic and can be spread faster than the organization's formal communication channels. Mishra (1990) further states, "the grapevine is also capable of penetrating even the tightest security because it cuts across organizational lines and deals directly with people in the know."[67] Organizations should not ignore rumors in the workplace that have the potential to harm its brand/image. This being said, organizations need to take

Professional Magazine, 4(2), 64-63. doi:http://dx.doi.org/10.1109/MITP.2002.1000472.

[64] Ibid.

[65] Hunter, B. (1983). Rumors: Pruning the Grapevine. *Today's Office.* Vol. 18, Issue 5.

[66] Hirschhorn, L. (1983). Managing rumors during retrenchment, S.A.M Advanced Management Journal. 48, Summer 1983, 4-11.

[67] Mishra, J. (1990). Managing the grapevine. *Public Personnel Management*, 19(2), p. 52.

responsibility and address rumors in the workplace before the situation becomes out of control.

Rumors abound in office conversations. Although 90% of employees are usually passive listeners, 10% take gossip seriously and are said to be active links in the passage of information.[68] Rumors in the company may contain different types of topics. But rumors in the workplace tend to focus on three most prevalent categories: on the quality of someone's work, tenure (whether or not someone's keeping their job] and personnel changes. Rumors are outcomes of interpersonal relationships. Research indicates that rumors among employees result from an organizational structure that frequently exposes employees to role conflict and ambiguity. Thus, a company with a "toxic" organizational culture can be prone to office rumors. The higher is level interpersonal conflicts in the company; the higher would the level of office rumors. In addition, employees experience rumors because of conflict between the instrumental and expressive functions that they perform."[69]

When employees spend work time speculating about the latest rumor, productivity suffers, and rumors can hinder interdepartmental cooperation. They can also harm a company in the marketplace. However, rumors can be an outlet for pent-up emotions, and they can help to maintain one-to-one contact"[70] One study revealed that rumors could be revenge in the workplace. Using hypothetical scenarios to manipulate organizational treatment of an employee and the believability of a rumor, the study showed that participants had higher intention to transmit a harmful rumor when the organization broke job-related promises (i.e., breached the psychological contract)

---

[68] Hunter, B. (1983). Rumors: Pruning the Grapevine. *Today's Office.* Vol. 18, Issue 5.

[69] Akanda, A., & Odewale, F. (1994). Company rumor: The fact and fiction. *Employment Bulletin and IR Digest, 10*(3), 1. Retrieved from http://search.proquest.com/docview/200259786?accountid=33657.
[70] Ibid.

and revenge played an import role in their motivation.[71]

Despite its destructive force in the workplace, a major percentage of employees considered rumors as the main source of information about organizational affairs. Since it is perceived by employees as a personal type of communication, it frequently has a strong impact on them than formalized channels of communication. The grapevine is much more flexible than formalized channels of communication. It is also a rapid source of informal news. After a "news" event occurs in an organization, the grapevine makes information available almost immediately[72]

Rumors also serve motivation goals. Rumors are often shared in the marketplace about products, services, brands or organizations; both in the online as well as in the offline scenarios. An exhaustive review of the literature identified four motivations for consumers to share rumors in the marketplace: anxiety management, information sharing, relationship management and self-enhancement.[73]

The existence of rumors during crises and uncertainties is a fact of life. "The good news is that preventive and remedial actions are

---

[71] Borgia, P. et al. (2014). Rumor as Revenge in the *Workplace. Group and Organization Management,* 39 (4): 363.DOI: 10.1177/1059601114540750. Retrieved from https://www.researchgate.net/profile/Robert_Tang5/publication/266384464_Rumor_as_Revenge_in_the_Workplace/links/545afe1a0cf2c16efbbbcf28.pdf.

[72] Akanda, A., & Odewale, F. (1994). Company rumor: The fact and fiction. *Employment Bulletin and IR Digest, 10*(3), p.28. Retrieved from http://search.proquest.com/docview/200259786?accountid=33657.

[73] Sudhir, S., & Unnithan, A. B. (2014). Rumors in the Marketplace: What Drives Them? In *AMA Summer 2014 Summer Marketing Educators Conference*. San Francisco, CA, USA: American Marketing Association.

possible, allowing professional communicators to minimize or even to stop the damage from rumors. Effectively preventing or controlling rumors requires an understanding of the psychological and sociological factors that drive people to listen to, pass along and believe rumors."[74]

6.3 How to Deal with Rumors in the Company

To help ensure happy endings to rumors at your organization, Kathy Fieweger, executive VP and general manager at MWW Group Midwest and national practice leader of the Enterprise Risk group, offers some advice on how to manage organizational rumors:[75]

1. Be aware of blips in your marketplace. Monitor all forms of media.

2. Prepare for four or five rumor scenarios. Draft key statements, and get legal involved in the process.

3. Figure out who your spokespeople will be, depending on the severity of the rumor.

4. Be smart in determining whether the rumor is a small wave or a tsunami.
5. Respond proactively, and ensure you're hitting the right media in the proper platform in response to the rumor.

6. Continue monitoring the marketplace for flare-ups once the rumor has subsided.

---

[74] Doorley, J., & Garcia, H. F. (2007). Rumor has it: Understanding and managing rumors. *Public Relations Strategist, 13*(3), 27-31. http://search.proquest.com/docview/204907950?accountid=33657.

[75] PR News, 67[38].

There are essentially three ways to manage rumor in a company.[76] The first is to try "to wait them out." Some rumors dissipate over time and do little harm. Only rarely are rumors serious enough to require action. Second, if waiting fails, the rumor must be publicly refuted. When the rumor is refuted and also made to look unreasonable in public it negates its "news value."[77] This strategy is the most straightforward and aggressive. The company (or other target) names the specific rumor and discredits its usefulness and the credibility of its source through an advertising campaign, a press conference or highly publicized event such as one used by a company while denying the accusation of promoting Satanism.[78] This technique is effective in making people disregard those still interested to pass the rumor along. Third, truth or authentic information should be released or positively advertised as swiftly as possible. The last point strives to associate the target of the rumor with positive features such as the company's traditional commitment to quality, excellence and consumer satisfaction. For instance, a Canadian brewery has used this strategy in strengthening the link between its company and positive features, while simultaneously at the same time dissociating the company and the rumor that is it owned by a Pakistani shareholder. Kaferer (1990) has suggested alternative, but not empirically acceptable, rebuttal strategies, such as creating counter-rumor and spreading disinformation."[79]

---

[76] Koller, M. (1992). Rumor rebuttal in the marketplace. *Journal of Economic Psychology*. 13 (1): 167-186.

[77] Shibutani, T. (1966). *Improvised News: A Sociological Study of Rumor*. Indianapolis: Bobbs-Merrill.

[78] Pettijohn, T.F. (1987). *Psychology: a Concise Introduction*.Guilford: Dreshkin Publishing Group.

[79] Akanda, A., & Odewale, F. (1994). Company rumor: The fact and fiction. *Employment Bulletin and IR Digest, 10*(3), p. 28. Retrieved from http://search.proquest.com/docview/200259786?accountid=33657.

If rumors seem to threaten the business organization, there are basically two ways to deal with them. The first is to try to prevent them. The supervisor must recognize that rumors have definite causes, most anchored on the lack of information about things important to employees and on the insecurity and anxiety that go with them. Whatever the cause, it must remember that rumors are received and transmitted by people in terms of their biases. Thus, the general theme of the rumors may be maintained, but the details are often altered to serve vested interests. The second is to try to vanquish rumors if they already affect productivity, community relations, or interdepartmental cooperation. "In refuting a rumor, a manager or supervisor should release the truth as quickly as possible. If a rumor is not subdued or quashed quickly, employees will interpret later events in the light of the rumor."[80]

"Communications is the primary weapon in putting an end to unwarranted gossip. The company story must be put across in a positive light. The media appreciates quick, accurate, and thorough responses, which should be provided. Staff members should also be used to spread the truth. Other potential allies can be contacted and persuaded to help. The best way to dispel a rumor is to establish a policy regarding the problem and let everyone involved know about it. Appoint one person or office as the source of information for the media. Above all, always give reasons for failing to answer to the media."[81]

During moments of organizational restructuring where rumors bound, "effective change communication campaigns are said to reveal, rather than conceal, reduce uncertainty through collective planning, and proactively establish and maintain trust."[82]

---

[80] Ibid, p. 29.

[81] Horton, T. R. (1983). Rumors: A corporate communication crisis. *Security Management, 27*(6), 21. Retrieved from http://search.proquest.com/docview/231188092?accountid=33657.

[82] DiFonzo, N., & Bordia, P. (1998). A Tale of Two Corporations: Managing Uncertainty During Organizational Change. *Human Resource*

The methods of spreading rumors follow the development of communication technologies. The personal and face-to-face transmission of rumors has gradually being dominated by online and electronic transmissions through the Internet and latest ICTs. The use of the Internet has emerged as what Kim and Bae (2016) as an "omnipotent precious sword" to spread rumors to build or destroy products and services "faster than the light" in the cyberspace is now the major concern of companies and consuming public.[83]

6.4 How to Deal with Commercial Rumors

In responding to negative commercial rumors, an experiment recommended that the cultural background of the choice of spokesperson addressing rumors. The results of the study showed that consumers from Eastern and Western cultural backgrounds respond to a different manner to spokespersons addressing the commercial rumors. Their cultural backgrounds and values appear to influence their belief about the veracity of the source responding to the commercial rumors and their message. It recommended that market personnel consider consumers' and buyers' core values when developing strategies for and selecting sources for controlling commercial rumors.[84]

Management (1986-1998), 37(3-4), 295. Retrieved from http://search.proquest.com/docview/224316267?accountid=33657.

[83] Kim, I., & Bae, Y. (2016). Is the internet an omnipotent precious sword? the use of internet and the spread of rumors to south Korean combatants *. *Korea Observer, 47*(1), 139-165. Retrieved from http://search.proquest.com/docview/1788746056?accountid=33657.

[84]Kobinah, T., & Mizerski, D. (2003). The effect of cultural allegiance and values on the perception of spokespersons denying commercial rumors. *Asia-Pacific Journal of Marketing and Logistics, 15*(1), 39-50. http://search.proquest.com/docview/227362362?accountid =33657.

There are several rumor-handling techniques that intelligent salespeople can use:[85]

1. The first step upon hearing a rumor is to try to track it to its source before giving the customer a definite explanation. Salespeople often are not in a position to handle a rumor effectively, particularly if it has spread. Thus, many firms ask their salespeople to channel all rumors through the public relations or communications department.

2. Sometimes, anticipating a rumor is the best way to handle it. Telling people what is going on, whether they have asked or not, can calm a lot of fears about a company's future. Some rumors may require delicate handling and discretion.

3. In deciding how best to handle a rumor, good salespeople should consider whether the person conveying the rumor is a friend or a stranger. The direct attack often is the most effective way to demolish adverse rumors.

When employees spend work time speculating about the latest rumors, productivity suffers, and rumors can hinder interdepartmental cooperation. They can also harm a company in the marketplace. There are 3 main ways to manage rumor in a company: 1. Wait it out. 2. Publicly refute the rumor. 3. Release or positively advertise authentic information as swiftly as possible.[86]

6.5 Legal Approach to Stop Office Rumors

If rumors in the office which are damaging people remained unchecked, they could be more harmful than reality. Managers must be alert to rumors that can create a hostile work environment for the

---

[85] Pollock, T. (1987). Selling in the Face of Rumor. *The American Salesman.* Vol. 32, Issue 3.

[86] Akanda, A., & Odewale, F. (1994). Company rumor: The fact and fiction. *Employment Bulletin and IR Digest, 10*(3), 1. Retrieved from http://search.proquest.com/docview/200259786?accountid=33657.

subject of the rumors. The legal approach requires that managers and supervisors must squelch rumors of suspected wrongdoing at the very onset by investigating and filing appropriate cases against the perpetrators. Company wrongdoing can take many forms such as theft of company property, fraud, sexual harassment and various types of discrimination. Malicious rumors which can create hostile work environment can be prosecuted in any of the following common types of wrongdoing:[87]

6.5.1 Defamation.

Defamation is the most common form of malicious rumors. This can either be in oral form or slander or written form or libel. It occurs when an individual communicates something that is not true to a third person without any kind of privilege to do so.

6.5.2 Fraud or Misrepresentation

An employee can be sued for fraud or negligent misrepresentation if he or she states something as fact to an employee who relies on it when the statement is not correct, and the employee is harmed as a result. Thus, a supervisor can be liable for misrepresentation when an applicant relies on his or her information which is based on unfounded rumor there will be great opportunities for advancement because of a forthcoming infusion of money into the company and subsequently discharged as part of a massive layoff.

6.5.3 Invasion of Privacy

This can happen when a supervisor, for instance, disclosed confidential information as a result of workplace conversation. Unlike defamation, the communication may very well true; however, privacy rights forbid its communication.

6.5.4 Harassment

---

[87] Zachary, M. (1996). The office grapevine: A legal noose? *Getting Results ...for the Hands - on Manager, 41*(8), 6. Retrieved from http://search.proquest.com/docview/214235428?accountid=33657.

Failure to control the spread of rumors in the workplace can result in lawsuits. "A court may determine that the workplace constitutes a hostile environment in violation of employment discrimination statutes. For example, a company may be found liable in a sexual harassment case for failure to stop the circulation of rumors about a supposed affair between two employees that created an unpleasant work environment for the employees. In other cases, the courts may find firms guilty of harassment on cases based on race, religion, national origin, so forth...Persistent and widespread rumors that are unchecked by managers and supervisors can result in a judicial determination that the employee who is the subject of the rumors has been unlawfully harassed.

6.5.5 Emotional Distress

Using employment discrimination statutes, employees can sue people in the workplace for rumors under the theory of "infliction of emotional distress." Managers must be alert to stop rumors circulating in the workplace which can result in the hostile work environment or create emotional distress for the employees as this can result in lawsuits.

6.5.6 Disability Discrimination

An employee may successfully argue unlawful discrimination on the basis of disability if company managers had listened to incorrect workplace rumors that the employee had AIDS and discharged the employee on the basis of those rumors.

6.6 Summary

This chapter provided an overview on the nature of rumors in business organizations, particularly in the workplace, as well as some basics steps on how to deal with them concretely. Business managers have different recommendations on how to address the various types of company rumors that tend to disrupt business operations. But if company rumors become more malicious and destructive to the business organization, they have to choice but approach the court and file legal actions to stop them altogether.

7 FUNCTIONS OF RUMORS AND GOSSIP IN BUSINESS

7.1 Introduction

The power of rumor resides in its unpredictability, permeability, liquidity, and destructibility. Rumors affect all aspects and dimensions of social life: individual and societal, micro and macro, religious and secular. The spread of rumors can be likened to an epidemic. It can spread like an epidemic infectious disease. And this similarity is obvious, and long-recognized in both social science and epidemiology literature.[88]

Rumors affect a country's economy, whether developing or developed country from the Global North or Global South. In 1997, for instance, rumors on the resignation of Mr. Amnuay Viravan, Thai's finance minister, sent the Stock Exchange of Thailand, or SET, index down 3%, or 14.78 points, to 482.94, its lowest level in eight years. It further slumped the Thai baht in both domestic and

---

[88] Noymer, A. (2001). *The transmission and persistence of urban legends': Sociological application of age-structured epidemic models*. St. Louis: Federal Reserve Bank of St Louis. Retrieved from http://search.proquest.com/docview/1698039361?accountid=33657.

foreign trading, with swap premiums rising as resignation rumors prompted fears of a currency devaluation.[89]

Rumors also affect business and financial markets. Knowledge means power and control. In an investment environment where there are uncertainty and high level of risk, people resort to all sorts of unverified information to control the outcome of their business deals.

In recent years, some major businesses have suffered from rumors that caused significant financial and image problems. Rumors can travel quickly and undermine the company morale and, eventually, productivity. Rumors are difficult to trace and almost impossible to stop. It takes a concentrated effort to dispel a business rumor."[90]

Rumors are always flying in business and can change attitudes of firms and individuals alike. In large US corporations, public affairs specialists are charged with monitoring the internal grapevine and the external rumor mill. Companies are turning to "professional rumor-fighters," but their success is not guaranteed by any means. "In US corporations, public affairs specialists are charged with monitoring the internal grapevine and the external rumor mill. The chemical industry maintains a hotline called TERP (Transportation Emergency Reporting Procedure) to report on emergencies in the shipping of hazardous materials to keep the rumor market from going wild."[91]

---

[89] Wain, B. (1997, Jun 19). Thai finance minister plans to resign. *Asian Wall Street Journal.* Retrieved from http://search.proquest.com/docview/315620557?accountid=33657.

[90] Horton, T. R. (1983). Rumors: A corporate communication crisis. *Security Management, 27*(6), 21. Retrieved from http://search.proquest.com/docview/231188092?accountid=33657.

[91] Rowan, R. (1979, Aug). Where did that rumor come from? *Fortune, 100,*130. http://search.proquest.com/docview/213255799?accountid=33657.

7.2 Rumors and Financial Markets

Rumors can also influence stocks and financial markets. They can be deliberately used to move stock prices. Rumors can be so powerful in stock markets that people are trading futures based not on actual figures and facts but on rumors. In 1990, for instance, a flurry of rumors sent oil futures prices rallying Wednesday afternoon, pushing it briefly above $39 a barrel but settling at $38.57, a record high closing price. "Some rumors circulating through the exchange Wednesday had President Bush issuing an ultimatum to Iraqi President Saddam Hussein, while others had Saddam issuing an ultimatum to Bush. Other rumors had an aircraft being shot down in the Middle East, embassies being stormed by the Iraqis and even a Soviet coup. Petroleum futures had traded lower on Wednesday morning, as investors responded to an American Petroleum Institute report issued the night before that showed adequate supplies of heating oil and gasoline. The rumors started kicking in around midday and prices began soaring."[92]

When remaining unchecked, rumors can have a life of their own in business. Once a rumor spreads among stakeholders and the public, it often becomes the basis for a fact--even when it isn't a fact at all. "Rumors can cause severe pain to organization's financial system and reputation. In 1990, for instance, Tokyo stock prices fell as speculative shares were sold on rumors that financial authorities had begun investigating the possible stock manipulation behind recent stock price surges of Honshu Paper & Pulp" (Wall Street Journal, 1990, 04 Sept) . In October 2008, rumors that Apple CEO Steve Jobs had suffered a serious heart attack caused $9 billion in market value loss. In late September of this year, Morgan Stanley CEO James Gorman went on the offensive to dispel rumors that his company faced huge losses because of massive exposure to faltering European banks" (PR News, 67[38]). Moreover, the Adelaide Bank of Australia also lost more than $100 million of the institution's value after a false rumor surfaced from nowhere that it had asked the Reserve Bank of Australia (RBA) for cash to bolster its reserves in September 2007. Despite the RBA's statement denying such request,

---

[92] Journal Record, 1990, 27 September.

the bank's share immediately closed about 7 percent down—a rout that wiped away $111.7 million of the bank's value.[93]

Rumors can also collapse major investment banks leading to declining of a global economic superpower such as the United States. This can be with the failure of major investment bank such as the Lehman Brothers, whose dealings were part of the economic collapse in 2008. After news revealed that Lehman Brothers was in talks with a South Korean firm over buying a stake in their company, shares of the bank plummeted 45% (Agence France-Presse, 2008). Moreover, rumors and news on investment banks looking for buyers created fear within the investing community resulting in the massive-selling of holdings by investors. The rumors of the impending demise and losses of the major investment banks had impacted not only the stock market but also the larger economy of the US.[94]

A study of Laouiti, Habib, & Ajina (2015) evaluating the impact of takeovers rumors, a special type of financial rumors on the liquidity of target companies listed in the French stock market, showed that rumors could indeed affect the stock market. They noted that rumors takeovers on certain firms due to liquidity problems had resulted in abnormal values of prices and volumes in the stock market especially during their publication date in the media.[95]

---

[93] AAAP Genal News Wires, 2007, 19 September.

[94] Karasadiris, P. (n.d.). What Effect Do Rumors Have on Publicly Traded Sports Teams? http://webcache.googleusercontent.com/search?q=cache:8FZfEUorQE8J:www.albany.edu/honorscollege/files/Karasaridis_Thesis_Final_Version.docx+&cd=6&hl=en&ct=clnk&gl=ph.

[95] Laouiti, M., Habib, A., & Ajina, A. (2015). Impact des rumeurs d'offres publiques d'acquisition sur la liquidité : Cas des entreprises françaises cibles/Impact rumors of takeover bids on liquidity : The case of french firms target/Impacto de rumores de ofertas públicas de adquisición sobre la liquidez : El caso de empresas francesas meta. *Management International, 19*(2), 159-170,275,278,281. Retrieved from http://search.proquest.com/docview/1673353001?accountid=33657.

Because of the power of rumors to move stock markets, securities regulators are seeking means of deterring the deliberate spread of false rumors to influence stock prices. Overseas and in the United States, market authorities are seeking a means to curtail rumors. The UK's Financial Service Authority, for example, encouraged financial firms to adopt the best practices for handling market rumors. In a 2008 study of 50 financial firms, it recommended that companies should adopt formal guidelines and policies on rumors; provide adequate training; and provide adequate monitoring of firm's communications and trading.[96]

In financial market, rumors can deliberately used to move stock prices. They can be so powerful in stock markets that people are trading futures based not on actual figures and facts but on rumors. In 1990, for instance, a flurry of rumors sent oil futures prices rallying Wednesday afternoon, pushing it briefly above $39 a barrel but settling at $38.57, a record high closing price. "Some rumors circulating through the exchange Wednesday had President Bush issuing an ultimatum to Iraqi President Saddam Hussein, while others had Saddam issuing an ultimatum to Bush. Other rumors had an aircraft being shot down in the Middle East, embassies being stormed by the Iraqis and even a Soviet coup. Petroleum futures had traded lower on Wednesday morning, as investors responded to an American Petroleum Institute report issued the night before that showed adequate supplies of heating oil and gasoline. The rumors started kicking in around midday and prices began soaring."[97]

7.3 Negative Effects of Rumors to Currency and Big Business

Rumors do not only move stock markets but also the country's currency. Whether true or false, rumors can affect currencies. In late

---

[96] *Tax Management Financial Planning Journal*, Jul 14, 2009.

[97] Journal Record, 1990, 27 September.

1994, for instance, rumors had been circulating in Mexico over the imminent devaluation of its peso. Businesses simply ignored them. But the rumors turned out to be true. Thus, many paid dearly as they were caught holding large dollar debts. In this case, business paid a huge price for not heeding the rumors. But in 1995, the Mexican business paid the price too for believing rumors. On November 3, 1995, a wild rumor of an impending *coup de etat* diffused by a major news agency had caused widespread panic throughout the nation and pushed the peso to an overnight devaluation of more than 10 percent. In this case, the Mexican business reacted quickly and heeded this rumor even without confirmation by any of the news outlets. The rumor turned out to be false, but the damage has already been done.[98]

Not responding promptly and effectively to rumors even if they turned out to be false can also be disastrous to a company. Commerzbank AG of Germany in 2002, for instance, failed to immediately address malicious rumors that the bank was facing serious liquidity problems and that it was on the verge of bankruptcy. To put an end to the persisting rumors which have been going around trading floors for weeks, the bank's Chief Executive, Klaus-Peter Muller, sent a memo to bank employees categorically denying the rumor as well as launched a public-relations offensive to protect the company. But it was too late. Although Merrill Lynch, the source of the rumors, apologized to Commerzbank AG, the damage has been done. The rumors had pushed the bank's share price to 18-year lows, and its share price was nearly halved in the Frankfurt trading.[99]

Rumors can foretell the future and anticipate the incoming demise of business firms. Before the collapse of the investment bank Lehman Brothers, rumors abound about its declining financial status.

---

[98] Adler, I. (1997). Inside the rumor mill. *Business Mexico, 7*(11), 14-15. Retrieved from http://search.proquest.com/docview/197135726?accountid=33657.

[99] Souder, E. (2002, Oct 08). Commerzbank fights rumors about its financial condition. *Wall Street Journal* Retrieved from http://search.proquest.com/docview/398877289?accountid=33657.

The stock of Lehman Brothers has plunged 60% amid the rumors that it has serious financial trouble that nears bankruptcy. Instead of addressing the allegations, Lehman Brothers denied the rumors which turned out to be correct. But the damage is irreversible. The bank eventually collapsed.[100]

The rumors that have attracted the SEC's attention stem from early June. On June 3, Lehman stock fell as much as 14% amid rumors that the firm had borrowed money from the Federal Reserve, a signal it needed to go to the lender of last resort to raise money and shore up its financials. Lehman publicly denied the rumor.

Then, on June 30, Lehman's stock fell more than 10% on a rumor that Barclays was making a bid for the investment bank for about $15 a share, below its trading price at the time. The rumor didn't pan out.

A couple of weeks later, on July 10, the market was awash in rumors that Pimco, the fixed-income asset management company founded by Bill Gross, and SAC Capital, the large hedge fund managed by Steven A. Cohen, were pulling their accounts from Lehman. The investment bank's stock dropped as much as 21% during the day before rebounding after both Pimco and SAC said they continued to trade with the bank as usual.

The rumors that have attracted the SEC's attention stem from early June. On June 3, Lehman stock fell as much as 14% amid rumors that the firm had borrowed money from the Federal Reserve, a signal it needed to go to the lender of last resort to raise money and shore up its financials. Lehman publicly denied the rumor.

---

[100]Elstein, A. (1998, Sep 14). With the market in a nosedive, investment banks hit first. *American Banker* Retrieved from http://search.proquest.com/docview/249835456?accountid=33657.

Then, on June 30, Lehman's stock fell more than 10% on a rumor that Barclays was making a bid for the investment bank for about $15 a share, below its trading price at the time. The rumor didn't pan out.

A couple of weeks later, on July 10, the market was awash in rumors that Pimco, the fixed-income asset management company founded by Bill Gross, and SAC Capital, the large hedge fund managed by Steven A. Cohen, were pulling their accounts from Lehman. The investment bank's stock dropped as much as 21% during the day before rebounding after both Pimco and SAC said they continued to trade with the bank as usual."[101]

Rumors also affect big business such as multinational companies.

It is not known exactly how the rumor got started that Procter & Gamble Co. (P&G) is associated with satanism. Early in 1982, a rumor spread throughout the US that (P&G) corporate product trademark is a satanic symbol, signifying a company connection with satanism and that a P&G executive appeared on a nationally televised talk show and claimed satanic influence was responsible for his success. By June, P&G noted receiving more than 12,000 calls each month about the rumor; the company could not track down how the rumor got started, but it received reports of the story from all 50 states. Three nationally prominent religious leaders made public statements concerning the untruth of the rumor. In July, P&G took legal action to stop the stories. Suits were filed against several individuals for libel, circulation of false and malicious statements, and for calls for a product boycott. The company

---

[101] Scannell, K. & Craig, S. (July 28, 2008). Agency Subpoenas Focus on 4 Rumors That Hit Lehman. *The Wall Street Journal,* C1.

asked for court action to stop these people from further activity and for compensatory and punitive damages. A booklet was produced and distributed by P&G explaining the company's symbol. P&G believes that its public relations efforts on this matter - taken to the press, the pulpit, and the courts - will keep people from believing the rumors.[102]

"The devil is in the details of the company logo, the oft-relayed claim says. The familiar, human-faced half-moon symbol, accompanied with 13 stars, is said to be a mark of the devil and incorporates the supposedly evil number 666. A version of the rumor also claims a top executive was unusually forthright during a talk show interview and fessed up to the whole worshiping-Lucifer thing. He punctuated the confession to the host (the name of which has changed over the years to include Phil Donahue, Sally Jessy Raphael, and Oprah) with the statement: "There are not enough Christians in the United States to make a difference." Procter & Gamble isn't the only company to be slandered with claimed ties to the Church of Satan; McDonald's and Liz Claiborne have had to fight similar rumors."[103]

Rumors can result in panic buying. "With more recipients, both real and potential, the influence of rumors has also increased. When a strong earthquake hit Japan and destroyed a nuclear plant in March 2011, rumors forced Chinese shoppers rushing to supermarkets to purchase salt on the basis that this would protect their health from any fallout.[104]

---

[102] Cato, F. W. (1982). Procter & gamble and the devil. *Public Relations Quarterly*, 27(3), 16. Retrieved from http://search.proquest.com/docview/222502072?accountid=33657.

[103] https://www.thestreet.com/story/11285589/11/10-bizarre-company-rumors.html.

[104] Xie, H. (2013, Oct 16). Rumors flourish in vacuum. *China Daily* Retrieved from http://search.proquest.com/docview/1557524196?accountid=33657.

Rumors can also a country's financial status. In 1989, for instance, Britain's financial markets became nervous as rumors of insider-trading scandal involving a senior government official pushed down sterling and stock prices. Denials by Prime Minister Margaret Thatcher and by the target of the rumors, Transport Secretary Cecil Parkinson, helped the markets make a partial recovery. But the rumors began to take more concrete form in an expected television expose on insider trading.

The insider-trading rumors emanated from an Edinburgh newspaper, The Scotsman, and London's Channel 4 Television, and played on market fears of more turmoil in the Thatcher government. With Britain's economy struggling, the government still is trying to recover from last week's resignations, over policy differences, of Chancellor of the Exchequer Nigel Lawson and Sir Alan Walters, Mrs. Thatcher's chief economic aide.[105]

7.4 Positive Functions of Rumors to Business

Many people may think that rumors and gossip are always negative because they are unfounded or half-truth and destructive of peoples' reputation and honor. Business management books often overlook the positive uses of rumors and gossip in business organizations. In fact, it is rarely discussed in business. However, there are instances that rumors and gossip can be helpful to business or everyday life. A person or group just needs to be creative on how to turn rumors and gossip into something positive when pursuing his/her personal or group interest. Moreover, rumors and gossip can be indicators of organizational culture of a particular business firm. The quantity and quality of rumors and gossip perpetuated in a business organization can speak a lot of its corporate culture.

A study by Thompson (2009) showed that rumors could aid in

---

[105] Rustin. E. (1989, Nov 03). U.K. market hurt because of rumors of insider scandal --- transport chief gossip sends pound and stocks lower; turmoil in government. *Wall Street Journal* Retrieved from http://search.proquest.com/docview/398127268?accountid=33657.

advertising products especially during their pre-release. It showed that the word of mouth behaviors differs markedly between pre-release and post-release. Prior to release, consumers showed a similar willingness to spread positive rumors about a new product—even when they possess a social identity based on a rival brand. However, following release, such consumers can show a lower willingness to share positive messages about rival brands relative to messages about their brands.[106]

7.2 Structural Problems Supporting Rumors and Gossip in Business Organization

It is normal in any business organization to hear rumors against the company, managers, supervisors as well as fellow employees. Unlike gossip, rumors deal with social issues, not personalities, that affect a sector of a company or the entire business organization. People may immediately dismiss rumors as hearsay and unproductive talk. But if they persist, they might have a structural basis that requires a closer examination and analysis. A persistent rumor about the company or workplace usually has structural roots that need attention and solution. All companies which face bankruptcy or imminent demise are always forewarned by rumors. Before Enron collapsed, for instance, rumors about the company fraudulent accounting persisted. But it seemed that the early warning signs were ignored by the company leading to its closure. "A detailed look at the Enron accounting scandal reveals the circumstances that made it possible for Enron to succeed in deceiving the public. There was connivance with external auditors & banks, while SEC gave Enron exemptions from investment laws, instead of paying heed to the early warning signs"[107] Persistent rumors and gossip in the company may indicate the following structural problems:

---

[106] Thompson, S. A. (2009). *From rumor to release: Leveraging social identification in marketing strategy* (Order No. 3351519). Available from ABI/INFORMGlobal.(304845513). http://search.proquest.com/docview/304845513?accountid=33657.

[107] http://www.brighthub.com/office/finance/articles/101609.aspx.

7.2.1 Lack of Transparency

A company which hides some vital information to their valued customers, stockholders, employees and to the public is prone to rumors. In today's social media age, it only takes a post, selfie, or viral video to spread the rumors if a business firm is found deceiving the stockholders or customers about the true state of the company, products or services. As the saying goes, "If there's a smoke, there's fire!". The smoke is the rumor, the fire is the negative effect that destroys the company. A firm cannot hide the reality to the public. It is only a matter of time that the fire will come out and burn the entire house! So, if there's a persistent smoke or rumor, it is better for house managers or CEOs to put it off before it burns the company. And this could only be done if the company starts providing clear and convincing information to the affected sector about the issue. A transparent system is less prone to rumors. Thus, when rumors came out about the bending of iPhone 6, Apple immediately issued a statement and credible explanation to stop the rumors on the alleged defects of the phone. And it did apparently succeeded in putting off the smoke as Apple posted a historical profit of $18 billion last year due to massive sale of iPhone 6 and iPhone6 plus.

7.2.2 Management Problem

Rumors and gossip -- whether positive or negative -- can be a diagnostic tool for managers and supervisors to feel the general pulse of the company. The gossip that circulates within an organization is an indicator of what employees feel and think about the business organization.[108] It is important that managers must be empirically updated with what's going on in the company. It there is a discontent in the company, the manager must be the first to know it, not the last one. S/he must be open to suggestions and willing to listen even to people whom s/he dislike. Rumors can serve as warning signs and guide for managers on what management area that s/he needs to examine and improve. A feedback mechanism is therefore necessary

---

[108] http://career-advice.monster.com/in-the-office/workplace-issues/good-office-gossip/article.aspx.

to check once in a while the general sentiment of employees in the company as well as the true state of things in the company. This feedback must come from below, from rank-and-file employees up to the top managers in order that the general picture of true state of the company will come out. The Japanese firms which use the inductive method of management are good on this. They usually ask feedback or opinion from people below before they create or implement a major policy that affects the entire business firm.

Remember: A persistent rumor can be an allay not an enemy in business when used wisely by business managers. They serve as a guide or indicator on what area to improve on in the company!

7.2.3 The Existence of Power Cliques

The persistence of rumors and gossip in an organization such as business firms or schools can also indicate the existence of powerful informal groups of employees or/and managers which control the information and management system of the company to their favor. One must always remember that information is a powerful resource which can be utilized by people to others. In a "toxic"cultural environment of an organization or business firm, it is oftentimes a network of powerful cliques or informal groupings of employees or/and managers that sow intrigues, rumors or gossips against any perceived enemies or competing individuals and groups within the organization. Sometimes the rumors and gossip are structured by the power elite to maintain their access and control of the perks and privileges in the company at the expense of others. In one Catholic college which this author used to teach, some lay managers and employees aligned by friendship formed informal alliances usually intrigues against their perceived enemies. Since most members of the network occupied managerial positions as program chairs, they had constant contact with the top management and they immediately create and report whisper to the vice-president any infraction of rules committed by some employees who were not friendly to their alliance. Rumors and gossip usually come from leaders or members of a powerful social network against the weaker ones. The weak and the powerless, in turn, would also create their rumors and gossips of resistance at the back the powerful. In other words, the intensity and scope of rumors and gossip in an organization is an indicator of power struggle between two or more opposing groups or networks within a social organization. Thus, if there is a high degree of rumors and gossip in a business firm, it suggests of power cliques vying for control of the company's resources.

7.3 Summary

This chapter has shown that rumors can have negative and positive effects to the economy, financial markets, currency, business operation and organization. Because of the unpredictability of business and financial markets, rumors abound that can negatively affect the various aspects of business. They can affect stock prices, financial systems of banks and business organizations. They also influence purchasing patterns of people and can collapse large investment banks such as the Lehman Brothers. Despite these negative effects, rumors can also provide positive effects to business such as providing a glimpse of the company's culture based on the quantity and quality of rumors as well as aiding the advertising of products. Rumors thrive in business if there is a lack of transparency in daily business operations and if the business organization faces serious management problems.

8 SOME CRITICAL ADVICE ON HOW TO DEAL WITH RUMORS AND GOSSIP

8.1 Introduction

This chapter aims to give some advice to people on how to avoid or minimize rumors and gossip in their everyday life. The advice is classified according to the source or cause of the rumors and gossip. They must be taken with caution since people belong to different cultural background. What works in one situation or to a particular person or group may not necessarily works in another situation or group of people. But societies and cultures also share some common cultural traits or what is called as cultural universals. Thus, the advice here is to some extent applicable only to many societies with advanced urban culture.

8.2 Advice on Physical Appearance

The most common target of gossip is people's appearance. People have different cultural taste and standards of what beautiful and appropriate in particular situations. Race which is based on physical traits such skin color, nose, height, blood type, makes people different from others. The white Caucasians or Caucasoid of Europe and North America, for instance, are different from the Asians or Mongoloid in height, skin, nose and other physical characteristics. Race is inborn, This is normal since so people can do much about it except by using the modern technology of cosmetic surgery to change their physical looks. There is much awareness of equality despite racial differences. But there are still abundant situations where people are racist and discriminate people based on the physical traits. Rumors and gossip can therefore thrive in a racist environment, where people's character and capability are judged based on their looks and or physical traits.

Discrimination and circulation of rumors and gossip can also thrive in situations even if people in an organization belong to the same race or cultural heritage. This happens when the person or group appears different from what is considered culturally appropriate, normal and acceptable.

8.2.1 Try to Associate with People with Similar Traits.

One of the most common ways to be targeted by rumors and gossip is to live differently from others in appearance. To be different in one's looks is an obvious way to get noticed and gossiped by inconsiderate others as deviant. This includes physical or racial traits such as height, skin color, hair, form of limbs, etc. How we look and present ourselves to others is our personal brand to use a marketing term. It's true that people judge books by their covers. In real life, people judge others from what they see externally if they don't understand people's motives especially if they are unfamiliar with the person.

People with physical disability usually experience a lot of demeaning rumors and gossip by people who do not understand their predicament. That is why children with special needs are better taken cared of if placed in an environment which addresses their peculiar needs—that includes the absence of persistent and humiliating rumors and gossip in the community. The statistical theory in deviance says that if a person, trait or condition does not follow the normal standard in society, then s/he is deviant. Thus people who are deaf, mute, blind, and with deformity are usually labeled by others as deviant because their physical traits are considered abnormal, below the normal traits of ordinary people. No matter how broad is the campaign against bullying and discrimination against disabled or physically challenged persons, there are always bullies or inconsiderate people who make fun and spread nasty rumors against people with handicap.

There are 3 possible ways to overcome bullying, rumor-mongering or gossiping against people with physical defects:

8.2.1.1 Place them in a Special Environment with People of Similar Physical traits.

This is the most common approach for people or parents who have the means to send their children or relatives in schools and institutions which can take care of their special needs. This includes school for the blind, deaf or mute, home for the aged or disabled children, orphanage, and others. The major problem in this case is the adjustment of the physically-challenged person once they leave or graduate from these institutions and interact with the public. They can't avoid hearing rumors, gossip or discriminatory remarks from inconsiderate people. In this case, the state must legislate laws which impose a stiffer penalty against discrimination of disabled persons in any form.

There are some establishments which hire people with similar physical disability such as massage parlors operated by blind people, factories with mute workers, restaurants with harelip waiters, etc. Disabled people can be spared from unnecessary rumors and gossip from their normal co-workers if they work in a workplace suited for their physical disability.

8.2.1.2 Lobby for laws that protect physically-challenged people or sue the bullies or offenders if laws are available.

The handicap may be protected in special institutions against bullying and discrimination but not when they interact with "normal" people in mainstream society. If these people are not protected by a high social status, as discussed below, then they can easily be victims of humiliating remarks and gossip. Thus, it is important that general and special laws with tougher penalties against bullying of disabled persons are in place to protect the physically-challenged people from humiliating rumors and gossip.

8.2.1.3 Develop the Person's Talents and Improve his/her Social Status.

People with high social status can oftentimes overcome discrimination and nasty rumors and gossip. Status has something to do with the marketability of a person's skills as well as his/her credential and level of personal prestige. Social status can ascribed or achieved. People who are born with rich and famous parents can acquire ascribed status. Thus, the children of President John F. Kennedy or any famous leaders and celebrities inherited the high social stature of their parents. But the boxer superstar Manny Pacquiao of the Philippines acquired his high status through achievement in boxing. So people with physical disability but with high social status can be spared from frequent rumors and gossip compared to those who are poor and of low social status. In general, people tend to disregard the physical defects of people who have ascribed or achieved social status, those who are talented and who excelled in their own chosen field. One blind college poor student-scholar of one top private university in the Philippines, for instance, is not discriminated by her classmates and but instead respected because of her intelligence and brilliance in Math. In fact, she graduated *Summa Cum Laude* from the university despite being blind. Thus, her achieved high social status has protected her from the unnecessary rumors and gossip. Another way then to minimize or avoid rumors and gossips for people with physical disability is to develop their talents and excel in a particular field of endeavor to gain respect from the public and deflect their attention to the disability which can generate rumors and gossip.

8.3 Advice concerning Personal Trait and Practice

People who are normal with no physical defects still suffer from persistent rumors and gossip either because their attitude, character and behavior do not follow the prescribed rules and norms of a particular society, institution or organization, or they are stranger or new to the organization whose norms and rules are different from what s/he learned in his/her social upbringing. In both cases, the person who appears different or deviant would normally suffer rumors and gossip for not complying with the prescribed rules and social expectations of the organization. Thus, homosexuals or gays who try to exercise their gender rights in repressive organizations or countries could end up ridiculed by rumors and gossip by heterosexuals. But in a environment where homosexuality is the rule such as living in the gay capital of the world, heterosexuality becomes deviant and the target of rumors and gossip. In other words, the prevailing culture and its norms and values can be the cause of labeling of people and the spread of rumors and gossip. In this case, a person can avoid rumors and gossip either by obeying and adjusting to the norms and cultural expectations of the social environment or migrate to a friendly environment. Filipino migrant workers in Europe, for instance, are criticized and gossiped by their employers and foreign friends for taking a bath everyday which is a practice in the Philippines but may not be in cold countries. In this case, migrant workers can go ahead with their cultural practice if they can; otherwise, they need to adopt the prevailing practice or work in their native country or to a country with similar hygienic practice.

8.3.1 Solicit Feedback from Friends to Improve One's Self.

People have blind spots. Once in a while it is better to ask some trusted friend to give an honest feedback about one's appearance and grooming as well as one's attitude towards others if these bother the person. The looking glass theory says that others are our mirrors on how we look at ourselves. Thus, it is better get a honest feedback from others in order that we can eliminate some sources of gossip in us. It things can be fixed through human effort, go ahead! If it only takes going to a beauty parlor to change your hair style to stop the gossip or remove a mole in one's face—why not if it buys you peace of mind! In other words, if it is within our means to fix things up to stop or minimize rumors and gossip, let us not hesitate to do it. Cosmetic surgery is morally acceptable if it enhances your personhood and life chances and not for vanity.

8.3.2 Take Gossip as a Constructive Feedback

Gossip can be interpreted as a constructive feedback to improve one's self. If the source of the gossip is your physical and personal traits, the solution is within your reach. Go and consult with a cosmetic surgeon, dermatologist, fashion designer, religious adviser or personality coach to improve your self. Gossip is also a constructive criticism from others about some undesirable personal traits. The Looking Glass Theory of C.H. Cooley (1964) in Sociology states that the other is your mirror in order that you can see your self objectively.[109] So it is important to listen to constructive gossip and do something to change these gossips into a means to achieve admiration and social acceptance.

8.3.3 Avoid a Highly-Politicized Organization

If your social upbringing is conservative and less political, then avoid a group or company whose organizational structure is highly politicized. If this is not possible, then join a power clique or group in the company which is more aligned with your personal principles or religious values to get group support and to survive in the business firm. But if you aim to maximize your benefits from the company, then join a power group which has a strong connection with the top management or owner/s of the firm who could be an ideal choice. There are basically two kinds of political groups in a highly politicized business environment: the pro-administration which are aligned with power holders and the anti-administration which are identified with social resisters and opposition groups in the company such as a critical labor union. Choose which group can be protect and promote your personal interest.

8.3.4 Avoid Remaining Silent

---

[109] Cooley, C.H. (1964). Human Nature and the Social Order. New York, NY: Schocken Books.

Silence may not always be the wisest cause of action in dealing with rumors and gossip—of course, trivial things do not need to be dignified with an answer. If the allegation is serious and persistent and the person or party concerned remained silent, people would start to think that the gossip is true. It has been said that silence means (tacit) yes—unless, of course, the rumor or gossip is true and victim just wants to let it be. But this will not stop the rumor from mutating and spreading. People would usually demand that they want to hear the truth directly from the horse's mouth. Statements from spokespersons are often unconvincing to the public. Spokespersons would just can make a spin to hide the truth and would just provide excuses or give his/her opinion in a press conference to protect their boss. In media interviews, the spokesperson is actually interpreting or giving his/her opinion of what the boss would probably say in public.

Tiger Woods faced the public and addressed the rumors and gossip about his extramarital affairs directly and thus allowed the issue to rest. If one is a popular businessman/woman or a celebrity, it would be wise to clarify things directly and honestly in a public statement, press conference, tweet, post or interview with the media. Tim Cook, the CEO of Apple, is another example that the heat of gossip is unbearable, it is better not to be silent. Just speak out and simply just tell the truth and the truth will set you free!

A manager can call a formal an looking for informal meeting with subordinates to clarify some vague policies or issues which fueled the rumors or gossip. A frequent, clear and convincing information with what's going on in the office, workplace or any area or division of work is a sure formula to kill rumors and gossip. Managers must be friendly and always in dialogue with their subordinates who cannot cope up with difficult tasks in order to avoid grumbling and intrigues. Being legalistic and fault-finder is a sure path for managers to create discontent to employees which lead to rumors and gossip. As already mentioned, rumors and gossip are "weapons of the weak" which they subtly use to retaliate against their "abusive" boss.

8.3.5 Always Provide a Regular and Convincing

Information

Rumors and gossip are most likely to spread when there is a lack of clear, frequent communication between management and workers.[110] (Seidenfeld, 2013). They thrive in situations of uncertainty, doubt, and utter lack of information. Thus, the only way to counter rumors and gossips is to provide a clear, frequent and convincing information about the personal or public matter that is being intrigued in order that people would not further speculate and imagine things to enlighten their ignorance or lack of knowledge. Doubt and uncertainty can provide an opportunity for resisters and haters to exploit the situation to their advantage and to destroy the person or system they dislike. Rumors and gossip are tools of social resistance for people who are dissatisfied with their managers, leaders, or co-workers or with the state of things or management they are in. They may seem trivial or insignificant. The celebrity, CEO or manager can immediately dismiss them as nonsense. But if the allegations are serious and are not responded to promptly and satisfactorily by the parties involved, rumors and gossip can spiral into a bigger overt or covert group protest and mass action. The dissatisfied can convince their colleagues to join their cause. Indeed, rumors and gossips can topple regimes and companies if not handled effectively. They can destabilize companies and wreck havoc to people's career and plans.

8.3.6 Use Rumors and Gossip to Identify the Firm's Problems.

Before blaming people, managers or administrators must instead first view and use persistent rumors and gossip as a guide in knowing what's wrong in their organizations or business firms. Rumors and gossip are raw an unverified information. However, if they are analyzed and processed correctly, their social patterns would emerge and tell a lot of the recurring problems in the organization. As already

---

[110] Seindenfeld, Martin (2013). "Workplace, Gossip and Rumors". http://www.alnmag.com/articles/2013/10/workplace-gossip-and-rumors.

mentioned, companies which became bankrupt were forewarned by rumors and gossip and yet no drastic and effective measures are undertaken by top management.

8.3.7 Reshuffle People to Minimize the Influence of Power Cliques.

If the corporate culture is personalistic, i.e., social ties matter more than merits, and lax in law enforcement or social control, influential power groups among employees and managers, competing to control the company's resources and rewards, are more likely to arise. The group which has more allies or connections with the top management would emerge as the hegemonic or most powerful elite group. Within a division or sector in a company, power cliques can also arise. To promote their group interest, these cliques would usually use rumors and gossip as a tool to undermine the system, their competitors, or to whoever blocks their way. The task for the CEO or manager of the company is to identify these power cliques and their leaders and to break their control and network. To minimize their negative impact to the company's goals, s/he must reassign or reshuffle them, making sure that their networks in the company cannot further create more politics and difficulties for others in the workplace.

8.3.8 Behave Discreetly.

The reactivist definition of deviance states that if you are not caught and condemned by the public for breaking the law or social norm, you're not a deviant, criminal or immoral.[111] If the immoral or criminal act is done in secret and no one reveals it, there would be no nasty rumors and gossip about it. Rumors and gossip are indicators of rule-breaking actions. So if the deviant act is hidden then there would be no rumors and gossip. Politicians who were exposed in public for wrongdoing because some people or events revealed their immoral or illegal acts.

---

[111] Goode, E. (2011) *Deviant Behavior*, 9th edn. Upper Saddle River, NJ: Prentice Hall.

Thus, if one wants to do something fishy or deviant and avoid rumors and gossip, s/he better do it in a secret or discreet way. Of course, doing something against the rules secretly is still deviant. Applying the normative definition, there is still deviance even if done secretly as a social norm has indeed been violated. The main difference between covert and overt deviance is, of course, the absence of humors, gossip and public condemnation in the former if the act is done discreetly.

Technology, particularly the digital and ICT technologies, is a great provider of anonymity and hiding for deviance in order that people can avoid rumors and gossip and ultimately public condemnation and punishment. Online prostitution transaction between the customer and the prostitute, for instance, is more difficult to detect than a face-to-face negotiation.

Anonymity in the use of technology is tone major reason why it's difficult to punish some bullies especially in the social media and cyberspace. They are good in keeping their activities secret and anonymous through creative use of evasive techniques to hide their illegal and immoral acts.

8.3.9 Live a Moral, Honest, Upright, and Generous life!

The best way to avoid humors and gossip is to live a moral, honest and upright life. People with many vices and hidden transgressions are prone to rumors and gossip. Just do your duty efficiently and be friendly to all in the workplace, not just your friends in the workplace. Greet or give them gifts or cards on their birthdays! Treat them to a light snacks if you get a bonus. The point here is to create a "debt-of-gratitude" to every person in your social environment. In general, people "don't bite the hands that feed them" or create gossips and humors to their benefactors or people who care for them. Be friendly to your enemies. Find means to befriend them and turn them into allies. If you can discover your their need or weakness where you can best help them, you're on your way to transform them as your friends. An enemy who becomes a friend can be a powerful ally especially if s/he has many followers!

If you are a manager or in position of authority, exercise your power judiciously and don't go beyond the limits of the authority given you by the company. Abuse of power attracts social resistance from subordinates. They may not show their opposition or resistance to your domination directly and overtly for fear of sanction, but they can show it indirectly through rumors and gossip to put you in a bad light, hoping that a higher authority can notice it, and eventually fire you from your job! Play by the rules and be fair in implementing them as a manager.

Rumors and gossip in public and corporate life illustrate that power is not possessed by people but exercised through the use of right strategies and tactics. Rumors and gossip are strategies of power and resistance. To avoid their negative effects to one's public or professional life, One must also be creative and think of ways to counteract rumors and gossip in a proactive way and convert them into occasions for personal and professional growth in business or in public life!

8.3.9 Turn Enemies into Friends and Allies

The best way to minimize rumors and gossip in your life is to turn your enemies into friends and allies. Take a look at this testimony of a person who turned his enemy into a friend:

> Early in my career, I was once figuratively stabbed in the back by a colleague, which nearly led to me being fired...Rather than waste time and energy by dragging around a bag of resentments, I worked on my negative attitude...Whenever we ran into each other, I would smile and say "Hello, how are you?" I was met with a scowl or ignored. This continued for three months, but I was determined not to let the person ruin my day. I no longer wanted to give away my power. Then, suddenly, my adversary had a change in attitude, and became a trusted associate.[112]

---

[112] http://www.bizcoachinfo.com/archives/11502.

Try active non-violence and apply the biblical teaching of loving your enemies. It is not a sign of weakness and cowardice of trying to win the hearts of your gossipers and rumor mongers. If you believe in something supernatural and have a solid philosophy in life, loving your enemies is a sign of courage and ultimate wisdom. After all, we are only pilgrims of this earth. Let us condemn and sue those who spread unjust and malicious acts of rumors and gossip. Let us condemn the acts but forgive the person as every individual can also be a victim of his/her past and social environment.

8.4 Summary

This chapter provided some critical advice to those who endure serious rumors and gossip in the workplace and everyday life. Rumors and gossip can come from different places because of one's peculiar physical appearance, traits, and attitudes. The type of place or organization can also make one looks different and abnormal. If one can do something with one's looks, then gossip can be minimized. If not, then one must find an environment where one's physical disability can be accepted. A highly-politicized environment is prone to rumors and gossip. Rumors and gossip must generally be seen as constructive in order to improve the self and one's company. Following the rules and living an upright life is always an antidote to rumors and gossip. Finally, turning enemies into friends is a very important strategy to fight rumors and gossip in everyday life.

ABOUT THE AUTHOR

Dr. Vivencio (Ven) O. Ballano is Associate Professor V of the Sociology Department of the Polytechnic University of the Philippines (PUP) in Manila. In 2011, he obtained his doctoral degree in Sociology from the Ateneo de Manila University. He was chosen Post-Doctoral Research Fellow of the Southeast Asian Studies Research Exchange Program (SEASREP). He is the author of the books "Law, Normative Pluralism, and Post-Disaster Recovery" and "Sociological Perspectives on Media Piracy in the Philippines and Vietnam," published by Springer Nature Singapore in 2016. Dr. Ballano's specialized areas of teaching and research include sociology of law, rumors and gossip, religion, disaster management, corporate organization, and the Catholic Social Teaching. Follow him on Twitter @detectivebogart.

www.ingramcontent.com/pod-product-compliance
Lightning Source LLC
Chambersburg PA
CBHW020924180526
45163CB00007B/2876